PRESERVING FIRE

PRESERVING FIRE

SELECTED PROSE

PHILIP LAMANTIA

EDITED AND WITH
AN INTRODUCTION
BY GARRETT CAPLES

BIBLIOGRAPHY
BY STEVEN FAMA

WAVE BOOKS
SEATTLE/NEW YORK

PUBLISHED BY WAVE BOOKS
WWW.WAVEPOETRY.COM

COPYRIGHT © 2018 BY ESTATE OF PHILIP LAMANTIA
COMPILATION AND INTRODUCTION COPYRIGHT © 2018 BY GARRETT CAPLES
BIBLIOGRAPHY COPYRIGHT © 2018 BY STEVEN FAMA
ALL RIGHTS RESERVED

WAVE BOOKS TITLES ARE DISTRIBUTED TO THE TRADE BY
CONSORTIUM BOOK SALES AND DISTRIBUTION
PHONE: 800-283-3572 / SAN 631-760X

LIBRARY OF CONGRESS CATALOGING-IN-PUBLICATION DATA
NAMES: LAMANTIA, PHILIP, 1927-2005.
TITLE: PRESERVING FIRE: SELECTED PROSE / EDITED BY GARRETT CAPLES;
BIBLIOGRAPHY BY STEVEN FAMA
DESCRIPTION: FIRST EDITION. | SEATTLE : WAVE BOOKS, [2018]
IDENTIFIERS: LCCN 2018004690 | ISBN 9781940696706 (TRADE PBK.)
LC RECORD AVAILABLE AT HTTPS://LCCN.LOC.GOV/2018004690

DESIGNED AND COMPOSED BY QUEMADURA
PHOTOGRAPHS APPEAR COURTESY OF THE ESTATE OF PHILIP LAMANTIA
PRINTED IN THE UNITED STATES OF AMERICA

9 8 7 6 5 4 3 2 1
FIRST EDITION

THIS BOOK IS FOR NANCY J. PETERS

PHILIP LAMANTIA IS NOWHERE TO BE SEEN.

—JOANNE KYGER and LARRY FAGIN

Lettre de Paris (1977)

"PRESERVING FIRE"
An Introduction to the Prose of Philip Lamantia

xv

Letter to Charles Henri Ford

1

Surrealism in 1943

5

The Tchelitchew Cover

8

Young Poets

9

An American Opinion

13

Conscientious Objector's Statement

16

Letter from San Francisco

21

Editorial from *The Ark* (1947)

28

Conscientious Objector's Statement II

31

Two Introductions to John Hoffman

35

Hymns to St. Geryon (1959) by Michael McClure

41

Biographical Note in *The New American Poetry, 1945–1960*

42

Vision and Instigation of Mescaline 1961

43

The Beat Generation

46

Mental Cement

49

RevelatNewsPort by Raphael Kohler

51

Notes Towards a Poetics of Weir

62

Testament of the Inter-Voice

68

Introduction to *The Wounded Mattress* (1970) by Sotère Torregian

70

Philip Lamantia

72

Statement for *Contemporary Poets of the English Language* (1970)

75

Between the Gulfs (with "By Elective Affinities, Then and Now")

77

Vital Conflagrations

79

The Crime of Poetry

80

Harmonian Research
82

The Oneiric Light of Alice Farley
83

Poetic Matters (with "Notes Toward a Rigorous Interpretation of Surrealist Occultation")
85

Invisible Webs
101

Gerome Kamrowski: The Revelation of Night
103

Radio Voices: A Child's Bed of Sirens
104

The Future of Surrealism
121

Alice Farley: Dancing at Land's End
124

Marie Wilson
126

Clark Ashton Smith Plaque Dedication
127

Statement on "Howl"
131

Letter from Egypt
132

Preface to *Crossroads of the Other* (1992) by Ken Wainio
140

Program Note from a Reading at the
Poetry Project at St. Mark's Church, April 1999
143

Surrealism & Mysticism
145

Statement
149

Bibliography by Steven Fama
151

"PRESERVING FIRE"

An Introduction to the Prose of Philip Lamantia

> *I suspect the general "linguistic" definition of poetry as "a certain highly concentrated language"—in contradistinction to the "more loosely concentrated one of prose"—to be generally correct, insofar as one can recognize the poetry as such even if it were presented as "conventional prose."*
> —PHILIP LAMANTIA, "Notes Towards a Poetics of Weir"

Philip Lamantia (1927–2005) was a major American poet, if not the preeminent American surrealist of the twentieth century. To say that prose was not his primary pursuit is therefore self-evident—assuming the conventional distinction between it and poetry—and yet there are poets for whom prose is a vital part of their writing. A poet like Lamantia's friend and contemporary Robert Duncan required two volumes and 1,200 pages of his *Collected Writings* (California, 2012–2014) to accommodate his prose. Lamantia was not that kind of poet. He was more like a Mallarmé, a poet with enough for one slim volume of prose, *Divagations* (Bibliothéque-Charpentier, 1897), and that an eclectic mix of decisive poetic statements and oddball occasional pieces. Even the diffident Mallarmé exceeds Lamantia's output, and at least had the luxury of personally assembling his own collection.

That Lamantia was both unwilling and unable to attempt such an editorial project seems incontrovertible. A poetic prodigy who began publishing in avant-garde periodicals at age 15, the young Lamantia soon quit high school and moved to New York in 1944 to live within the war-exiled surrealist milieu. Though he obtained a high school diploma after his return, and spent much of 1947–49 auditing courses at the University of California, Berkeley, he expressed to me on more than one occasion regret for his lack of a more conventional formal education, feeling it hindered his ability to write prose. This is, in some sense, absurd, given the vast extent of his erudition; he was quite possibly the most educated person I've ever encountered and could discourse freely on a bewildering variety of subjects, for hours at a stretch. Yet even here, he was easily inhibited by the presence of a recording device and he was a notoriously difficult interview, leading me to conclude that his problem with expository prose had less to do with any imagined educational deficiency and more with his exacting standards for correctness.

Like Mallarmé's, some of Lamantia's prose has an occasional quality, the composition of a given piece dictated by circumstance. Items devoted to individual poets, for example, include important associates like Michael McClure, John Hoffman, Sotère Torregian, and Ken Wainio, but leave out other equally significant comrades like Bob Kaufman, Will Alexander, Ronnie Burk, or Laurence Weisberg. Texts devoted to individual artists like Gerome Kamrowski, Marie Wilson, or Guy Harloff are equally the result of chance and opportunity, overlooking such key associates as Bruce Conner, Harry Smith, Wallace Berman, or Kurt Seligmann. There are no less than three short statements about surrealist dancer/choreographer Alice Farley, which is odd simply as a matter of proportion in his slender prose output.

And too, there are whole areas of Lamantia's enthusiasms his prose barely touches on, or not at all. Like many poets of the Beat Generation, among whom he is frequently placed, Lamantia had a significant relationship with jazz, championing a whole constellation of musicians from Charlie Parker to Cecil Taylor to Ornette Coleman, and virtually none of this appears in his prose. His interest and expertise in alchemical texts from Flamel to Fulcanelli hardly surfaces, and his intensive, years-long study of Egyptology and sacred geometry, his encyclopedic knowledge of West Coast Native American myth and culture, and arcane studies in heretical Christian mysticism are but briefly alluded to. Troubadour poetry, cabala, the cultivation of wheat(!)– many of Lamantia's intellectual obsessions are missing here, or so fleetingly indicated as to belie their importance to him.

Nonetheless, despite its incomplete snapshot of the pursuits, despite its inconsistencies and self-contradictions and necessarily posthumous nature, Lamantia's prose, taken sequentially as a whole, constitutes not only a vital book in itself but also a thumbnail intellectual biography of one of the major American poets of the twentieth century. Without recapitulating the biographical introduction I co-wrote with Andrew Joron and Nancy Joyce Peters to the *Collected Poems of Philip Lamantia* (California, 2013), what I'd like to do here is relate some circumstances around the composition of these prose works in order to illuminate their meaning, in the words of Joseph Conrad, "as a glow brings out a haze."

*

The earliest writings here stem from Lamantia's first encounter with surrealism, all the more extraordinary for having been written between the ages of 15 and 17. The first three are letters, and the letter, with its mixture of formality and informality, will remain among the primary vehicles for his prose. The undated "Letter to Charles Henri Ford" was written in April 1943, according to an editorial gloss of the one fragment of it published in the June issue of *View*, a glossy avant-garde quarterly edited by Ford and Parker Tyler. Five poems by Lamantia would also appear in that issue of *View*, making him one of only two contributors to emerge from the pile of unsolicited submissions.[1]

1. The other, Joe Massey, was an incarcerated murderer.

Aside from the aforementioned fragment, this letter's never been published, yet it's an invaluable record of Lamantia's trajectory through surrealism leading up to his first publication. In 1943, the amount of surrealist writing and writing on surrealism in English was limited, and Lamantia managed to hit most of the available texts, listing both David Gascoyne's prose *A Short Survey of Surrealism* (Cobden-Sanderson, 1935) and his poetry *Hölderlin's Madness* (J. M. Dent, 1938); Georges Lemaître's academic treatise *From Cubism to Surrealism in French Literature* (Oxford, 1941); the 1940 *New Directions* annual with its extensive surrealism section; Alfred Barr and Georges Hugnet's *Fantastic Art, Dada, Surrealism* (MoMA, 1936); and Ford's own *The Overturned Lake* (Little Man, 1941). Interesting is what is missing—Julien Levy's *Surrealism* (Black Sun, 1936), though Lamantia names this text in his 1998 interview with David Meltzer in *San Francisco Beat* (City Lights, 2001)—as well as the inclusion of *Several Have Lived* (Gemor, 1942), an unconvincing stab at surrealist poetry by journeyman litterateur Hugh Chisholm made plausible by the inclusion of three tipped-in drawings by André Masson.² Perhaps most intriguingly, Lamantia cites Peruvian surrealists César Moro and Emilio Adolfo Westphalen, whose work he encountered in *An Anthology of Contemporary Latin-American Poetry* (New Directions, 1942).³

The letter is remarkably sophisticated given Lamantia's youth, and if there's the faintest whiff of juvenilia, it's gone by the next selection written six months later, a letter to André Breton published, along with three poems, under the title "Surrealism in 1943" in the final double issue of the official organ of the Paris surrealist group in NYC exile, *VVV*. Dated October 8, 1943—19 days before Lamantia's 16th birthday—the letter is arguably the first U.S. surrealist manifesto, even as it modestly presents itself as a clarification of the young poet's "relation to surrealism."⁴ "To rebel!" Lamantia writes. "That is the immediate objective of poets!" Breton's presentation of Lamantia is telling, including a classically surrealist headshot of the young poet and giving pride of place among the poems to "The Islands of Africa," dedicated "To the memory of Arthur Rimbaud, the rebel and the seeker ..."⁵ Clearly, Breton is positioning Lamantia as a contemporary Rimbaud, and Lamantia seems willing to step into this role.

The final two pieces from Lamantia's earliest period would appear in *View*. "The Tchelitchew Cover" is no doubt another fragment from a longer letter, appearing in the March 1944 issue and commenting on the painting by Ford's partner Pavel Tchelitchew, *The Flower of Sight* (ca. 1943), which appeared on the cover of the December 1943 issue. In it, Lamantia expresses profound admiration for the painting, which he characterizes with the paradigmatic surrealist epithet "marvelous." The timing here is noteworthy,

2. Chisholm, incidentally, had previously appeared in *View*.

3. I owe this information on the source of Lamantia's encounter with the poetry of Moro and Westphalen to Lamantia bibliographer Steven Fama (Email from Steven Fama, 5/1/17).

4. David Meltzer, "Philip Lamantia (1998)," *San Francisco Beat* (City Lights, 2001), 135.

5. *VVV* no. 4 (February 1944), 19.

appearing a month after Breton's embrace of Lamantia's work on behalf of the surrealist movement, for despite Ford's repeated entreaties, Breton did not extend the same approbation to Tchelitchew's art.

The following month (April 1944) Lamantia would arrive in NYC, remaining there for the rest of the year working as an editorial assistant for *View*. During this period he writes his first proper essay, "Young Poets," a review of the third installment of New Directions's *Five Young American Poets* (1944), including Ecuadorian Alejandro Carrión and U.S. poets Jean Garrigue (misidentified as "he"), John Frederick Nims, Eve Merriam, and Tennessee Williams. Of the five, only Carrión receives any praise—and even that qualified—from Lamantia, who otherwise excoriates the young Americans. The teenage surrealist declares the "verse" of the rest "adds nothing to the poetry of the new generation," reserving an especial scorn for Tennessee Williams. Given that Williams's first major theatrical success, *The Glass Menagerie*, would only open on Broadway at the end of March 1945, in other words, shortly after the publication of "Young Poets," the critique seems rooted in purely poetic terms, unaffected by considerations of fame or success. Indeed there's no reference to Williams as a dramatist whatsoever.

What Lamantia chiefly objects to among the four U.S. poets is the shoulder-shrugging triviality that runs through their statements on poetics, whereas his own such statement in *VVV* indicates that, for him, poetry was a matter of life or death: "At the present time when the forces of extreme principles are being felt almost by the whole world, a true revolutionary poet cannot help defying every appalling social and political instrument that has been the cause of death and exploitation in the capitalistic societies of the earth. If he is one for the transformation of the world, as he should be, and if he is not stupid, in relation to a method of approaching these vital issues, the poet will not be opposed to the Surrealist attitude." If there is one constant among Lamantia's varying poetics, it's the surrealist notion that a poetics implies a way of life.

Disillusioned with the NYC surrealist milieu and having broken with Ford (though remaining on the masthead of *View* for another year), Lamantia returned to San Francisco by the end of 1944. Presumably written before his departure, "Young Poets" would appear in *View*'s March 1945 issue. By November of that year, a new, more explicitly politically engaged Lamantia emerges in "An American Opinion," appearing in the November 3 issue of George Woodcock's London periodical *Freedom Through Anarchism*. In the eight months separating these publications, two major shifts have occurred. The first is a rejection of surrealism in favor of the influence of Kenneth Rexroth, affecting both Lamantia's thought and his poetry. The second, of course, is the August 1945 U.S. atomic bombing of Hiroshima and Nagasaki, Japan, a true paradigm shift in the calculus of warfare. For the first time, human beings had developed a weapon capable of ending life on Earth as we know it; certainly the threat of "The Bomb" cast its pall over the subsequent Beat Generation, though Lamantia's outrage here is chiefly directed at the "thorough disregard for human values" shown by the American media coverage of the death of so many civilians, the entire lack of "sympathy for these people (who were enemies only in the strict military sense)."

Lamantia's move from surrealism to anarchism reflects his participation in Rexroth's Wednesday night Libertarian Circle meetings, the poets at which "included Robert Duncan, Philip Lamantia, Jack Spicer, William

6. Michael Davidson, *The San Francisco Renaissance* (Cambridge, 1989), 38. According to Duncan biographer Ekbert Faas, "a surviving program leaflet," while omitting Broughton and Gleason, adds Sanders Russell and Muriel Rukeyser. See *Young Robert Duncan: Portrait of the Poet as Homosexual in Society* (Black Sparrow, 1983), 193.

7. Meltzer, *San Francisco Beat*, 136.

Everson, James Broughton, Thomas Parkinson, Madeline Gleason, and Richard [O.] Moore"[6]—the beginning, in short, of what would come to be known as the San Francisco Renaissance. Lest we imagine such gatherings to be purely literary events, the Libertarian Circle meetings eventually numbered over 100 people, including older Italian anarchists and conscientious objectors, whose common denominator was a sense of social justice.[7] It was a bit of a movement, in other words, in the way that much subsequent Bay Area culture would be.

Under Rexroth's direction, the Libertarian Circle presented and debated anarchist thinkers like Kropotkin, Goldman, and Buber, and it fell to Lamantia to lecture on the politically infused psychoanalytic theories of Wilhelm Reich, whose *The Function of the Orgasm* (Orgone Institute, 1942) surfaces at the close of "An American Opinion." Reich's writings on, as Lamantia puts it, "the relationship between the political, moral, and social patterns in our society and their detrimental effects upon the individual's psychic life and in turn its effects upon these patterns," would prove influential among Beat Generation authors like William Burroughs and Jack Kerouac, and the appeal of Reich to an estranged admirer of Breton is obvious. Both had sought to achieve a union of Freud and Marx, taking the psychiatric illnesses of people in modern capitalist society as a sign of the need for its destruction and reorganization along socialist principles, before moving in a more anarchist direction. When Lamantia declares, moreover, that "[a]s a poet I can envision no other position of moral responsibility to myself and to others than a consistently revolutionary individualism—something that can only come in its own in the world, if Anarchism were established in the hearts of men," it is difficult not to see this as a further articulation of his declaration to Breton, "To rebel! That is the immediate objective of poets!"

Reich constitutes the primary link between "An American Opinion" and Lamantia's "Letter from San Francisco," published two years later in the October 1947 issue of Cyril Connolly's London-based magazine, *Horizon*. Taken on its own, "Letter from San Francisco" is an overview of the city's postwar literary and intellectual boom, and is perhaps the then-19-year-old Lamantia's most impressive prose effort of the '40s. Among the significant poets Lamantia highlights here are Rexroth, Everson, Duncan, Parkinson, Moore, Sanders Russell, Robert Stock, Janet Lewis, and Patricia Umsted,[8] as well as George Leite's magazine *Circle* and Bern Porter Editions, which had published Lamantia's debut volume, *Erotic Poems*, the previous year. But in order to appreciate its full significance, we must understand the "Letter" as a pointed refutation of an article by Mildred Edie Brady, "The New Cult of Sex and Anarchy," which appeared in the April 1947 issue of *Harper's Magazine* and is only mentioned in the penultimate paragraph of Lamantia's text. Brady's article and her follow-up, "The Strange Case of Wilhelm Reich," in the May '47 issue of *The New Republic*, almost single-handedly turned the tide of public opinion against Reich, who within weeks would find himself under FDA investigation. But while "The Strange Case" is a full-throated attack on Reich himself, "The New Cult" aims at the Bay Area's Reich-influenced proto-Beat bohemia, particularly as embodied by Rexroth's Libertarian Circle, as well as Henry Miller's followers.

As journalism—with its invented quotations, strawman arguments, and deliberate misrepresentations—"The New Cult" makes *Life* magazine's hatchet job on the Beat Generation 12 years later seem evenhanded.[9]

8. I have yet to turn up much information on Patricia Umsted. Janet Lewis, interestingly enough, was the wife of Stanford professor and antimodernist formalist poet Yvor Winters, though Lamantia misidentifies her book *The Earth-Bound* (Wells College, 1946) as *Bravery of Earth* (Jonathan Cape, 1930), the title of a book by Richard Eberhart. Eberhart was a friend of Lamantia's and wrote testimony on his behalf for his conscientious objector status, though their poetics weren't at all aligned.

9. See Paul O'Neil, "The Only Rebellion Around," *Life*, November 30, 1959.

Brady's rhetorical strategy is to portray the intellectual activities around Rexroth and Miller as passé, a rehash of the postwar ferment of the 1920s, but the smug tone is belied by the ill-concealed hysteria motivating a 7,000-word attack in a major national magazine. Lamantia himself isn't named in Brady's article, but he is specifically attacked as one of a "small group of Gnostic anarchists weaving together the elaborate mysticisms of the Gnostic heretics of the second century A.D. and the philosophies of both Kropotkin and Wilhelm Reich ... They are currently preparing a magazine to embody their views which has been named *Ark*, and which they are slowly printing by hand on an old press housed in a San Francisco basement."[10] *The Ark* was an attempt to launch an avowedly anarchist, *Circle*-style, avant-garde magazine edited by Lamantia along with Sanders Russell and Robert Stock, though it turned out to be a one-shot.[11] In "Letter from San Francisco," Lamantia dismisses Brady's attack as "Stalinoid," and though the poet's enthusiasm for Reich is somewhat tempered by a disavowal of "his theories of biophysics," Lamantia continues to affirm "the basic truthfulness of his findings."

Brady's identification of Lamantia as a "Gnostic anarchist" may be the most striking part of the above-quoted passage, for this is the first public association of him with any sort of religious identity. We can see, however, that Lamantia's religious interests began to surface in late 1945, under Rexroth's influence, as Lamantia makes an impassioned religious argument in his letter to the draft board declaring his conscientious objection to military service. It would be easy to be cynical about the timing of Lamantia's religiosity here, inasmuch as religious grounds are generally the primary criteria for achieving conscientious objector status, but this interpretation is

10. Mildred Edie Brady, "The New Cult of Sex and Anarchy," *Harper's Magazine* (April 1947), 316.

11. I've also included in this collection *The Ark*'s unassigned "Editorial" note, presuming it to be a collaboration among the three editors.

belied by both the poet's ongoing engagement with esoteric thought—predating even his encounter with the surrealists[12]—and his subsequent lifelong pursuit of spiritual enlightenment through his study of world religions. His religious beliefs are undoubtedly sincere, and one imagines the consternation of the draft board member who received such a letter, which goes back to the concept of original sin and runs through Thomas Traherne, D. H. Lawrence, T. S. Eliot, Nikolai Berdyaev, Reich, and Simone Weil. Several of Lamantia's friends—Rexroth, Stock, Moore, Richard Eberhart, and *View* co-editor Parker Tyler—also wrote letters on his behalf, preserved in his archive at the University of California, Berkeley's Bancroft Library, and, despite the serious stakes involved, the comic potential of the clash between the Libertarian Circle and the U.S. Army is perhaps realized in an anecdote about Lamantia's draft hearing Thomas Parkinson relayed to Robert Duncan, which Duncan subsequently wrote up in a letter to his friend Pauline Kael:

12. See, for example, Garrett Caples, "A Note on *Tau*," *Tau* by Philip Lamantia and *Journey to the End* by John Hoffman (City Lights, 2008), p. 8, n. 5.

> First witness for the defendant was Kenneth Rexroth who explained at some length and with his usual exceeding eccentricity the operation of Avatar and the Kundalini and the implications of cabalistic Christian esoteric religious belief in relation to war. Who was followed by Bob Stock who said in the wild-eyed wild-haired tradition of the Bohemian: "Of course Lamantia doesn't want to go to war. It's easy to explain. He comes from a long line of Italian anarchists. I don't want to go to war myself. I don't want to be invaded by the state." "WHAT DID YOU SAY?" asks the examiner in a gesture of ethical deafness. "INVADED BY THE STATE?" Who was followed by a letter from Lt.-Commander Richard Eberhart of the U.S.N.
>
> At which the draft board all nearly collapsed.

What do you do? they asked Kenneth Rexroth. I am a poet.

What do you do? they asked Bob Stock. I'm a poet.

Who is this Lt.-Commander Richard Eberhart? they asked Lamantia. He is a poet.

At which point Dick Moore took the stand.

What do you do? they asked Dick.

I'm a WRITER! he said gravely and triumphantly.

A WRITER, they echoed with some satisfaction (thank god not another poet).[13]

13. Faas, *Young Robert Duncan*, 197.

Despite—or maybe because of—the burlesque quality of this scene, Lamantia was granted CO status, though the question of his draft status would again be raised in 1949, in the build up to the Korean War. Lamantia's second statement of conscientious objection, while essentially restating the position of his 1945 letter, is at once more religious and less polite. The antistatist anarchism evident in 1945 is much condensed in favor of a straightforward invocation of the spirit of God—indicative of his increasing orientation toward Catholic mysticism that will culminate a decade later in his second book, *Ekstasis* (Auerhahn, 1959)—while his disgust with the increasing conservatism of American society at the dawn of the '50s makes his refusal to enter military service all the more brusque and dismissive.

The 1950s were a difficult decade for Lamantia, evidenced by the slender selection of prose. I should note the present volume excludes two prose texts published, with three poems and two translations, in the Auerhahn Press pamphlet *Narcotica* (1959), included in his *Collected Poems* so as not to unduly separate the contents of the former. But various circumstances in his life impacted his productivity during this period. In 1950, he began a dozen-year, off-and-on struggle with heroin addiction, reflected in *Narcotica*'s infamous cover of Wallace Berman photographs depicting Lamantia shooting up, and the draconian circumstances of the lives of addicts in American society form the subject matter of the pamphlet's opening manifesto, "I Demand Extinction of Laws Prohibiting Narcotic Drugs!" On the spiritual plane, Lamantia converted to Catholicism in 1955, and there is undeniably an inhibition created by the circumstances of his belief. The zeal with which Lamantia pursued spiritual orthodoxies—the correct belief, the right way to worship, the most efficacious path—paradoxically drove him to the unorthodox (viz., the aforementioned "Gnostic heretics of the second century A.D.") in quest of the truth. Lamantia was heretical never for the sake of it, but only when driven by spiritual necessity. But this concern for truth could be paralyzing, in the sense that he was rarely satisfied with any prose explication of his knowledge of a given subject. In assessing his output during this period, we must also allow for the fact that he burned most of his unpublished writing in 1960, during a spiritual crisis, and it's not unreasonable to suppose there were prose texts among these destroyed works. He was also twice deported from Mexico, where he spent much of the 1950s, losing many valuable books and papers in the process.[14]

Even as Lamantia retreated to an underground, nomadic existence, however, his immediate peers in age began to emerge as the Beat Generation, sparked in the Bay Area by the Six Gallery reading at which Allen Ginsberg debuted "Howl," on October 7, 1955. The reading, emceed by Rexroth, also included Gary Snyder, Philip Whalen, Michael McClure, and Lamantia him-

14. Garrett Caples, Andrew Joron, and Nancy Peters, "High Poet: The Life and Work of Philip Lamantia," in *The Collected Poems of Philip Lamantia* (California, 2013), xli.

self, who was reluctant to participate due to the spiritual distance he felt from his pre-conversion poems but relented on the condition that he read the poems of his close friend John Hoffman, who had died of unknown causes in Mexico in 1952. Hoffman is the subject of two short introductions, each written by Lamantia for separate attempts to publish an edition of his friend's poems, under the titles *Journey to the End* (Bern Porter Editions) and *Farewell Final Albatross* (Auerhahn Press), neither of which came to fruition. These introductions and Hoffman's poems wouldn't appear until 2008, under the title *Journey to the End*, as part of City Lights Pocket Poets No. 59. The third text from the 1950s, on McClure's *Hymns to St. Geryon* (Auerhahn, 1959), appeared as signed copy in Auerhahn Press's 1959 catalog. Lamantia here "reciprocated" McClure's text for Auerhahn's postcard announcement for Lamantia's second book, *Ekstasis*,[15] and, brief as it is, the "press release" is significant as an example of the more emphatic, exclamatory style—characterized by frequent passages in all caps—that dominates *Narcotica* and Lamantia's prose generally in the 1960s.

15. See Alastair Johnston, *A Bibliography of Auerhahn Press & Its Successor Dave Haselwood Books* (Poltroon Press, 1976), 10–12.

If anything symbolizes Lamantia's state of mind at the dawn of the 1960s, it would be his contributor note to Donald Allen's seminal anthology, *The New American Poetry 1945–1960* (Grove, 1960). While participants were given latitude to write up a significant statement, Lamantia barely musters 40 words, alluding to his surrealist past and his present, "mostly underground, and traveling." Not only did Lamantia burn his unpublished work at this point, he also decided to abandon poetry altogether, a resolution he fortunately did not keep. By October 1960, he will have completed the MS for his next book, *Destroyed Works* (Auerhahn), though production delays ensured that the volume wouldn't appear until 1962. In the interim, Lamantia produced two prose pieces published here for the first time. The first, "Vision and Instigation of Mescaline 1961," comes from an uncharacteristically clean typescript, indicating that it had achieved something like its final form, in contrast to other unpublished prose. Written in the emphatic style of the *Narcotica* prose, "Vision" is an exhortation to make mescaline "generally available in [the] USA" to promote visionary experience and spiritual enlightenment, a good six years before the Summer of Love. Lamantia was unquestionably a pioneer in Bay Area psychedelic culture, introducing peyote into the literary scene as early as 1951[16] and famously participating in the Washo Indians' peyote ceremony in 1954.[17] As the latter encounter suggests, Lamantia's esteem for mescaline—the active ingredient of peyote and hallucinogenic mushrooms—was inextricably bound to his restless spiritual quest; "Vision" characterizes mescaline as "revealing God in all things," and tellingly the manifesto is dedicated to his friend, the Nicaraguan poet and Catholic priest Ernesto Cardinal.

The second text—which I've titled "The Beat Generation"—is of uncertain origin. A letter dated "August 30, 1961," addressed to no one even as he's been "asked" to write it, the text is notable as the sole example of Lamantia positively placing himself under the Beat Generation rubric. Generally, and particularly in relation to his identification as a surrealist, Lamantia rejects the *Beat* label, or at most begrudgingly accepts the designation of "fellow traveler." But here he takes ownership of the concept, defining Beat primarily in relation to "the advent of the Bomb" and the countercultural rejection of American consumerism. His roster of Beat poets is idiosyncratic, beginning with ex-wife Gogo Nesbit and listing "John

16. John Suiter, *Poets on the Peaks: Gary Snyder, Philip Whalen & Jack Kerouac in the North Cascades* (Counterpoint, 2002), 114.

17. "High Poet," xxxvi–xxxvii.

Hoffman, John Wieners, Gregory Corso, Carl Solomon, Michael McClure, Gary Snyder, Allen Ginsberg, and Blackburn, Olson, and Kerouac," as well as visual artists Sheri Martinelli, Iris Brody, Ronnie Bladen, Bruce Conner, and Harry Smith. Indeed, Ginsberg's name is one of two handwritten emendations to the otherwise clean typescript, indicating the extent to which this Beat conception is distinctly Lamantia's. That is, his reluctance to name Ginsberg of all people in a list of Beat poets stems from their complicated relationship, for Ginsberg was an unwavering advocate of his work, and while Lamantia clearly benefitted from this, he remained ambivalent about Ginsberg's role as an impresario of poetry. Perhaps even more eyebrow-raising than his near-exclusion of Ginsberg is his inclusion of Charles Olson among those who have "made poetry GO *ON* since 1946," for his early appreciation of Olson's breath-based concept of "projective verse" will give way to a profound antipathy toward the Poundian poetics of *The Maximus Poems* during Lamantia's 1970s association with the Chicago Surrealist Group. The occasion of this letter, as well as whether Lamantia sent it, remains unknown.

The next two texts postdate *Destroyed Works* and find Lamantia in Morocco, during a 1964 visit to Paul Bowles. The presumably unpublished "Mental Cement" pays homage to Dutch visual artist Guy Harloff, best known as the discoverer of the famous "Beat Hotel," that Paris headquarters of Beat artists like Burroughs, Corso, Ginsberg, Brion Gysin, and Harold Norse. The second, "RevelatNewsPort by Raphael Kohler," stems from the same period, though wasn't published until 1968 in the *International Times*. A decidedly un-PC indictment of the repressive political situation in postcolonial Morocco and a manic rant about the country's prison conditions, following a five-day stint for possession of kif, "RevelatNewsPort" is the apotheosis of the emphatic prose style originating in *Narcotica*, and represents the final bleak moment of Lamantia's exile from the surrealism of his youth. The return to surrealism in 1965—under the influence of his relationship with his future wife Nancy Peters, whom he met that year—brings both a new calm and a new authority to Lamantia's prose, shedding the manic excesses of the prior decade.

Written circa 1965, "Notes Towards a Poetics of Weir" is a transitional text as Lamantia moves back into surrealism. Ostensibly a letter to Robert Hawley, the publisher of Oyez Press, who would bring out an edition of Lamantia's early surrealist poems under the title *Touch of the Marvelous* in 1966, the previously unpublished "Notes" seems to have been intended as either a preface or afterword to the book, judging from the several drafts in Philip's archive and an early table of contents to the book in which the text is listed. Lamantia begins to develop his idea of "weir" in the late 1950s—as it first appears in *Ekstasis* and persists through *Destroyed Works*, making its final appearance in "Gork!" from his 1967 *Selected Poems* (City Lights)—and it's notable as one of his few attempts to synthesize a concept as opposed to discovering one through his researches. What he means by it is not precisely clear; in "an ambitious, heavily worked, but ultimately abandoned text, 'Weir-o-Rama,'" Lamantia provides a "dictionary-style definition": "weir: anglosaxon: 'weird,' from Latin & Greek: TO SEE in a certain 'light[.]'"[18] This doesn't, of course, make literal sense, as Anglo-Saxon derives from an entirely distinct branch of Indo-European from Latin and Greek. As my co-editors and I wrote in the introduction to his *Collected Poems*, weir seems to be Lamantia's "attempt to correlate his ex-

18. "High Poet," xliii.

19. *Ibid.* periences of mystical, drug-induced, and poetic vision under one heading."[19] Still, I'm not entirely sure this earlier definition is consistent with the one appearing in "Notes": "For it is in the rapport of 'things different from one another' that the poet reveals & communicates his vision commingling the visible & invisible, the heard & unheard, seen & unseen, intuitive and cerebral knowledge, the concrete & abstract; hence: the purely sensorial level of apprehension connected to the *inborn, instinctive, cordial* & *supra/harmonic* levels of understanding (prophecy) which *are weir*, a designation/emblem of analogy, a homonym/translation derived from the Latin word 'to see' (vidi)!" The new emphasis here on analogy—a keynote of postwar surrealism—no doubt reflects Lamantia's renewed involvement with the movement, and soon enough he will abandon weir in favor of more orthodox surrealist concepts like automatism.

Lamantia's transition back to surrealism feels more complete by 1968's "Testament of the Inter-Voice," another unpublished text in which he explores automatism as "a kind of absolute knowledge which refuses cerebral & rational forms of comprehension but which *living poetry*—poetry *lived*—may reveal; by imaginative transmutation, a poem or image—painted, sculpted or written—gives testament and is a sign of direct knowledge-in-being." That same year, Lamantia returned to America after six years' wandering through Spain, France, Italy, Greece, and Morocco. The next text in this collection, his "Introduction" to *The Wounded Mattress* by Sotère Torregian, a New York School surrealist transplanted to the Bay Area, was written in Seattle, where Lamantia lived with Peters while she obtained a library science degree from the University of Washington. Though brief, Lamantia's introduction finds him stepping into the role of surrealist past master, in the Breton-like position of declaring surrealism much as the older poet once welcomed him into the movement as a teen. This is followed by an eponymous text drawn from a brochure entitled *The New American Poetry Circuit* (1970), published by a San Francisco booking service for college campuses looking to host prominent poets. In this context, Lamantia's page-long statement is one of the most expansive, as though making up for the terse bio in the actual *New American Poetry* anthology. Perhaps most significant here is Lamantia's own diagnosis of his "long interior odyssey" following his original surrealist period as a teen, which "now seems no more than a reaction against the impact surrealism had for [him] originally," and his dismissal of his Catholicism as "this strangest contradiction to poetry." This text is followed by a brief excerpt from what was almost certainly a longer statement written for the massive reference book *Contemporary Poets of the English Language* (St. James, 1970), in which Lamantia reaffirms his allegiance to surrealism in terms not terribly unlike his initial 1943 statement on the matter.

For Lamantia, in terms of his prose, the 1970s begin in earnest with his rapprochement with the Chicago Surrealist Group. The Chicago group was founded in 1966 by left-wing poet-activists Franklin and Penelope Rosemont—who had worked with the Industrial Workers of the World and Students for a Democratic Society—after a visit the previous year to Paris, where they'd met André Breton and participated in the surrealist movement's café meetings. Lamantia had gotten hold of the first issue (1970) of the group's irregular magazine *Arsenal/Surrealist Subversion* and soon contacted them to join forces, one of several artists historically connected to

Breton's movement to do so.[20] Lamantia was particularly active with the group, at times exclusively appearing in the pages of its publications, and eventually being listed as a contributing editor to *Arsenal*. Unlike his encounter in New York with organized surrealism in the '40s, when he was at its periphery, Lamantia was a central figure with the Chicago group even from distant San Francisco, the successive publications of *Touch of the Marvelous*, *Selected Poems*, *Penguin Modern Poets 13* (1969),[21] and a volume of entirely new work, *The Blood of the Air* (Four Seasons, 1970), establishing his reputation as the preeminent U.S. surrealist poet. While he left the running of the group to the Rosemonts, Lamantia quickly settled into the role of its acknowledged authority on surrealist poetics, resulting in his most productive period as a writer of prose.

"Between the Gulfs," with its pendent declaration of "Elective Affinities"[22] to surrealism and to *Arsenal* specifically, is Lamantia's opening salvo as a member of the Chicago group, appearing in the second issue in 1973. In this short statement, he discusses working on "a group of poems bearing the title *Becoming Visible*," which would indeed be the title of his next new book, though it wouldn't appear until 1981. Intriguingly, he takes the occasion of this pledge of allegiance to not so much rebuke as warn the group in terms of its poetic output. He asserts that writing is "a rigorous reconstruction against the past.... [W]e can all the more happily trace our inspirations from Lautréamont and Rimbaud to Breton and Péret and Roussel to Magloire-Saint-Aude, exemplary signposts for further transgressions, without literally re-tracing in one's own poetic praxis their inimitable movements." Lamantia was clearly concerned about the group's poetry, seeking to avoid rehashing surrealism as a particular and/or historical aesthetic

20. Among these artists we might list such significant surrealists as Clarence John Laughlin, Leonora Carrington, Gerome Kamrowski, Mary Low, and E. F. Granell. Though Breton himself died mere months after the group formed, the Chicago surrealists definitely had the sanction of the Paris group, if not always its approval in the matter of pronouncements.

21. Here he is sandwiched rather oddly between Charles Bukowski and Harold Norse.

22. I should note that the "pendent" section "By Elective Affinities, Then and Now" was later reprinted as a separate piece from "Between the Gulfs" in *The Forecast Is Hot!: Tracts & Other Collective Declarations of the Surrealist Movement in the United States 1966–1976* (Black Swan Press, 1997), but based on both the table of contents of

with its own attendant clichés. Such concern was perhaps a counterweight to the doctrinaire approach of group leader Franklin Rosemont, who generally took an orthodox Bretonian position in relation to surrealism. "Between the Gulfs" is followed that same year by the brief "Vital Conflagrations," first issued in the Chicago group's *Bulletin of Surrealist Information*, in which Lamantia introduces the alchemical and hermetic concept of the "Great Work" into his discourse; originally referring to the transformation of the *prima materia* composing the four elements into the philosopher's stone—a mythical substance thought capable of transforming base metals into gold—the Great Work came to symbolize the attainment of spiritual enlightenment, which was the concept's primary sense for Lamantia. Though part of Lamantia's poetry from the beginning, the language of alchemy and hermeticism takes on an increasing role in his subsequent work.

By 1974, Nancy Peters was working for Lawrence Ferlinghetti in the editorial offices of City Lights Books, eventually becoming co-owner of the combination bookstore and press. That year Ferlinghetti edited and published *City Lights Anthology*, the last 50 pages of which contained a special self-edited section by "The Surrealist Movement in the United States," featuring work by the Chicago group as well as by Bay Area associates of Peters and Lamantia like Laurence Weisberg. The final piece in the *Anthology*, save for "Harmonian Research," an invitation to fellow surrealists to get in touch, is Lamantia's two-paragraph statement, "The Crime of Poetry." Taking as his starting point early-nineteenth-century French poet and Neo-Pythagorean Antoine Fabre d'Olivet's derivation of the word "poetry" from Phoenician as "*the superior principle of language*," Lamantia argues here for the surrealist conception of poetry as "an instrument of knowledge, of

Arsenal 2, which only lists "Gulfs," and Lamantia's article-concluding "signature," which only appears after "Elective Affinities" but not after the main body of "Between the Gulfs," I'm forced to conclude that these are in fact one single piece.

discovery, of unveiling, and of human freedom," as opposed to the "debasement and fragmentation of language by reason," which he associates with "the monstrosity that was Ezra Pound, [and] his worthless emulators." Here we should note that the *City Lights Anthology* opens with excerpts from Allen Ginsberg's 1967 journal of "Encounters with Ezra Pound," in which the "Howl" author depicts himself offering his "blessing" to the disgraced modernist innovator:

> "But I'm a Buddhist Jew—perceptions have been strengthened by the series of practical exact language models which are scattered thruout the *Cantos* like stepping stones—ground for *me* to occupy, walk on—so that despite your intentions, the practical effect has been to clarify my perceptions—and, anyway, now, do you accept my blessing?"
>
> He hesitated, opening his mouth, like an old turtle.
>
> "I do," he said—"but my worst mistake was the stupid suburban prejudice of antisemitism, all along, that spoiled everything—" This is almost exact.
>
> "Well no, because anyone with any sense can see it as a humour, in that sense part of the drama—you manifest the process of thoughts—make a model of the consciousness and antisemitism is your fuck-up like not liking Buddhists but it's part of the model as it proceeds ..."[23]

23. Allen Ginsberg, "Encounters with Ezra Pound: Journal Notes," in *City Lights Anthology* (City Lights, 1974), 14–15.

With its insistence on the "moral" objectives of surrealism, "The Crime of Poetry" is a direct repudiation of Ginsberg's contribution to the postwar rehabilitation of Pound, the continuing attempt to insulate him from his own racism and active support of Mussolini during the Second World War. That Lamantia links this critique to poetics via the difference between Poundian and surrealist conceptions of language sets the stage for one of

his most fully realized prose essays, "Poetic Matters," appearing two years later in *Arsenal* 3.[24]

Written under Hegel's conception of poetry as "unfettered imagination" and Bachelard's insistence on the poetic image as a "*de*formation," "Poetic Matters" denounces vast swaths of postwar American poetry as fundamentally corrupted by their relationship to Pound's poetics. Citing Pound's acknowledged debt to Marinetti's futurism, Lamantia declares that:

> Contrary to the consensus of American literary "authorities" who decided to separate Pound "the man" from "the poet," deploring his fascist politics and hailing his literary achievements, I believe Pound's poetics are as anti-human as his politics and, if his poetry is examined closely, considering the historical facts vis-à-vis Marinetti's futurism, it will be obvious to what extent the two currents interpenetrate. Fascism's claim to "revolution" by the cult of "youth" and "newness" while resuscitating the classicist values of Greco-Roman civilization and concretized, laughingly so, in the architecture known as "Mussolini modern," is a neat similitude to Pound's exclusive and scholastic insistence on Aristotelian logic and his aping of "the classics" while cinematically employing the linguistic idioms of a political ward heeler in the United States of the 1920s.

This is Lamantia's prose at its most intense and concentrated, the heft of a dissertation distilled in two serpentine sentences. There's a gracefulness to this *je refuse*—in contrast to his vitriolic bombast of the '60s—that nonetheless conveys his full measure of scorn for the revisionist readings of Pound that continue to this day. "Poetic Matters" is particularly noteworthy for the way he links this condemnation of Pound's poetics to Charles

---

24. Like "Between the Gulfs" with its pendent section "Elective Affinities," "Poetic Matters" has a coda, "Notes Toward a Rigorous Interpretation of Surrealist Occultation," which was mistakenly reprinted as a separate piece entirely in *Surrealist Subversions: Rants, Writings & Images by the Surrealist Movement in the United States* (Autonomedia, 2002). Based again on the signature and the table of contents in *Arsenal* 3, thematic evidence like the recurrence of Hegel, and consultation with Nancy Peters, I have kept "Notes" as the ending to "Poetic Matters."

Olson, for where Lamantia felt enthusiasm for Olson's breath-based theory of projective verse a decade and a half earlier, he now decries the *Maximus* poet's "misappropriated scientific jargon"—"kinetics," "energy-discharge," etc.—as an unwitting return by way of Pound to futurism's exaltation of technology. He also singles out "Creeley, Ginsberg, Duncan, [and] Levertov" as "among the most voluble practitioners and theorizers" of this compromised poetics, with a general swipe at "post-Olson poets," by which I'm not sure he doesn't mean those later identified as Language Poets. Lest we imagine "Poetic Matters" is purely negative critique, however, he proposes the beginnings of an alternative American modernist lineage to the Pound-Eliot-Joyce canon in poets such as Samuel Greenberg, Harry Crosby, and Mina Loy, and identifies contemporaries who defy the Poundian legacy without formal allegiance to surrealism, like Gregory Corso, Bob Kaufman, and Daniel Moore. In addition to his invocation of the usual surrealist suspects like Breton, Lautréamont, Rimbaud, and Baudelaire, Lamantia touches on his recent experiences witnessing the ritual dances of the Hopi Indians in Arizona, seeing in their ceremonies the embodiment of "Hegel's definition of poetry as 'the universal art.'"

While "Poetic Matters" represents his definitive surrealist poetics of the 1970s, Lamantia's greatest turn as an essayist and arguably most original contribution to surrealist thought is "Radio Voices: A Child's Bed of Sirens." Published in *Cultural Correspondence*, a New Left magazine edited by Paul Buhle with a strong interest in pop/pulp material, in its Fall 1979 issue devoted to "Surrealism & Popular Accomplices," "Radio Voices" is Lamantia's analysis of the golden age of American radio (1920–1950), focusing on the oneiric imaginative states induced by the audio-only medium, as well as the influence of the "magico-mythic hero" (the Shadow, Chandu, Mandrake, and other radio magicians) on adolescent psychology. The piece draws on media studies and psychoanalytic studies of magic and combines them with elements of memoir, as Lamantia recalls his own childhood period of intensive listening between 1934 and 1942. He intriguingly locates his primary early exposure to poetry here in the pop cultural realm of radio, movies, and comics, in contradistinction to the moribund nineteenth-century poetic curriculum he encountered in San Francisco's public school system. It seems worth recalling the scarcity of such media materials as he discusses here at the dawn of the 1980s, well predating the current wealth of online availability. Lamantia is working largely from memory, in itself suggesting the powerful psychic impression left by supposedly disposable entertainment, and to me "Radio Voices" ranks among the crucial surrealist texts of pop cultural analysis, like Buñuel's "Variations on Adolphe Menjou's Mustache" (1928), Parker Tyler's fantasia on *The Maltese Falcon* (1941), or Breton's paean to silent film in *Nadja* (1928).

The period of Lamantia's active participation in the Chicago Surrealist Group more or less ends with the Summer 1981 issue of *Cultural Correspondence*, in which he and Nancy Peters contribute an untitled collaborative text, later known as "The Future of Surrealism," to a multi-author "Symposium on Surrealism." Acknowledging the fragmentation and collapse of the American Left at the dawn of Reaganism, "The Future" nonetheless reaffirms their faith in surrealism as a force for liberation which, much like communism in the face of Stalinism, has never really been attempted. Surrealism, they write, "is not dead," but rather "has yet to achieve conditions in which it can live for the first time." Nonetheless, "The

Future"—along with his third appreciation of Alice Farley, from the City Lights anthology *Free Spirits: Annals of the Insurgent Imagination* (1982)—finds Lamantia at the end of his decade-long pursuit of organized surrealism, as well as his most active period as a writer of prose. Surrealism will remain Lamantia's primary poetic touchstone for the rest of his life, and he will continue to connect with various practitioners including the Rosemonts and Bob Kaufman, as well as subsequent poets like Will Alexander, Ronnie Burk, and Andrew Joron. But generally speaking, his own practice—as well as his presence in American poetry—becomes increasingly hermetic from this point onward.

Though he will publish what is arguably his magnum opus, a final, entirely new volume of poems called *Meadowlark West* (City Lights), in 1986, the '80s are a thin decade for Lamantia's prose, represented here by a few odds and ends: his long-sentence-long contribution to the pamphlet accompanying Marie Wilson's 1984 art show in the basement of City Lights; his note for the *Annotated Howl* (Harper & Row, 1986), describing his 1953 Koran-induced vision of heaven that inspired the fifth line[25] of Ginsberg's "Howl"; and his unpublished "Clark Ashton Smith Plaque Dedication," delivered in Auburn, CA on the titular occasion and claiming the California symbolist and science-fiction writer for surrealism under the banner of black humor. But perhaps his most significant prose work of the decade was never intended for publication. "Letter from Egypt," as titled here, was written as a letter to Lamantia's ex-wife Goldian Nesbit and her husband André VandenBroeck, though it was never sent. The original, preserved in the Lamantia archive at the Bancroft Library, is a marvelous 10-page journal, hand-

25. To wit: "who bared their brains to Heaven under the El and saw Mohammedan angels staggering on tenement roofs illuminated[.]"

written on Egyptian hotel stationery, of two weeks exploring the temples at Luxor and Karnak with Nancy Peters. While the experiences he describes would ultimately form the basis of his most significant post-*Meadowlark West* poem, "Egypt," the letter itself is a valuable prose record of Lamantia's decades-long study of esoteric Egyptologist R. A. Schwaller de Lubicz.

Lamantia's interest in ancient Egypt stretches at least as far back as 1963, when he went to Nerja, Spain to visit with Nesbit and VandenBroeck. He hoped to learn more about Schwaller de Lubicz, with whom VandenBroeck had spent most of 1959 and '60 studying "sacred geometry" and the *symbolique*, which is "aimed at transcribing in a functional manner the esoteric significance of a teaching whose inner meaning remains inexpressible by any other form" and "eludes rationalization."[26] While VandenBroeck's focus was on the mathematical relations of architectural features of the temples and other sacred buildings, Lamantia experienced the symbolique—including the representations and functions of the *neter* (gods)—as directly relevant to his poetic and spiritual practice. Much of Schwaller de Lubicz's exposition of the symbolique is devoted to the esoteric significance of the architecture of Luxor Temple, derived not simply from its hieroglyphics but also from its orientation in relation to the cosmos and the location of and relationship among various features. These are read not in linear or contiguous fashion so much as in the juxtaposition of sometimes distant but parallel planes within the temple, hence Lamantia's letter is filled with discussion of the particular trajectories he and Nancy took through the complex in order to interpret one feature against another. The casualness of the personal letter, written to friends well versed in the rarified subject

26. R. A. Schwaller de Lubicz, *Sacred Science: The King of Pharaonic Theocracy* (1961), trans. André and Goldian VandenBroeck (Inner Traditions, 1982), 120.

matter, allows Lamantia to put forward his ideas without the inhibitions a more formal occasion might have incurred, while the weight of its erudition is leavened by observations on local cuisine, Egyptian tobacco, still-extant ancient agricultural practices, and even his terror of the traffic coming off Tahrir Square, making for lively reading.

The rest of Lamantia's ultimately modest prose output can be briefly summarized. The most substantial piece is a short "Preface to *Crossroads of the Other* (1992) by Ken Wainio." Wainio (1952–2006) was one of several poets around North Beach, San Francisco in the 1970s who were saddled with the unfortunate sobriquet "Baby Beats." Though ambivalent at best as an adult Beat, Lamantia was drawn to Wainio and his work by their connection to surrealism and to Egypt; Wainio's first book, *Letters from Al-Kemi* (Sombre Reptile, 1982), chronicles his own trip to Egypt ten years before Lamantia's. The most significant connection, however, in terms of this preface is Wainio's birthplace in California's Redwood Valley, 100 miles north of San Francisco, a region that had taken on great significance for Lamantia as the home of the Pomo Indians. While *Meadowlark West* provides evidence enough for Lamantia's obsession with Native Californian cultures and the Northern California bio-region, "Preface to *Crossroads of the Other*" contains his only prose devoted to the topic, which formed no small part of the poet's conversation in later life.

Not long after writing this piece, however, Lamantia—a lifelong manic depressive—fell into a deep depression lasting almost six years, virtually silencing his pen. But he would emerge for one final period of literary activity with the City Lights publication of *Bed of Sphinxes: New & Selected*

Poems 1943–1993 (1997), marking some 50 years as a publishing poet. In 1999, he made his final trip to New York City to read at the Poetry Project, and it is to this occasion that we owe the last of his several autobiographical summaries, a fax he sent to the Project that was reproduced in the program for the event. What is especially notable here is his restoration of Kenneth Rexroth to the chronology of his literary development, for Lamantia had essentially disowned this period of his life with his mid-1960s return to surrealism, feeling that Rexroth had led him away from the true path of his development. In this restoration, I think, he was influenced by his extensive 1998 interview with David Meltzer for the latter's book *San Francisco Beat: Talking with the Poets* (City Lights, 2001), in which he warmly recalled his former mentor.

The final two entries are products of my own instigation. In 2001, I was commissioned by a magazine to interview Lamantia, a piece that was ultimately rejected on the grounds of being "too esoteric" for mainstream consumption. It would appear after Lamantia's death in 2005 in Kevin Killian and Dodie Bellamy's venerable zine *Mirage/Periodical*, and has had its life online.[27] At this remove, given the intended venue necessitating a tediously oversimplified exposition of surrealism, the piece seems hardly satisfactory. Yet the actual Q&A is of value, documenting as it does Lamantia's late period of Catholicism, to which he returned after a 1998 mystical experience in North Beach's Shrine of St. Francis. This period is notable for Lamantia's simultaneous embrace of Catholicism and surrealism, a somewhat controversial stand, given the anticlerical stance of the latter. But Lamantia's surrealism was beyond anyone's strictures at this point. The bulk of our Q&A appears under the heading "Surrealism & Mysticism." Always a reluctant

27. Originally posted by Narrow House Recordings, with whom I recorded a poetry album in 2006, the interview still appears at the hoary old URL www.angelfire.com/poetry/thepixelplus/nhlamantia.html.

interview subject, Lamantia was clearly doing this as a favor to me, and our dialog here was generated by my taking notes over the phone, writing them up as his answers, and submitting them to him for correction. He was by no means fully satisfied with the results but graciously signed off as my deadline loomed. However, after the initial draft, he sent me two handwritten paragraphs which appear here as "Statement," which I promptly appended to the end of the piece as a suitable conclusion. I have separated this portion simply because it stands alone as an unmediated example of Lamantia's writing, distinct from assemblage-like answers of "Surrealism & Mysticism." And it still seems like a good way to end.

GARRETT CAPLES

SAN FRANCISCO
MARCH 20–JULY 4, 2017

PRESERVING FIRE

LETTER TO CHARLES HENRI FORD

Dear Mr. Ford,

Not to have this fact seem too important, in relation to my poetry, I state nevertheless that I am fifteen years old.

My recent verse can be considered Surrealist, though my very first poem expressed a longing for the unreal, the marvelous. Therefore a new plane of existence takes form, in my poetry, with the use of dream imagery and magical symbols. (This I realize is somewhat old stuff to you, and yet I want to speak of it.) A new psychial experience is viewed, where the dream thrives in its indigenous realm of fantasy. The words seem to lose their history, and they become free, a freedom in the sense of Hölderlin's or Rimbaud's paradise, and as André Breton has said: to make love.

I am sending you several of my most recent, and I believe my best, poems that you may possibly want to use in *View*.

I do not spring from the leisure class, in fact I am very far from it, and therefore I have not as much time to devote to my poetry as I would like to have. I do, though, confine all my energy, apart from school work (I attend one of those appalling public high schools) and other matters, to writing. If I am serious about any one thing, in its entirety, it is poetry. But I must be heard! I must be heard as soon as possible, for conditions as they are I will perhaps have to limit my attention to poetry in the future. But I will never stop writing it!

I hear so much criticism on my work, from teachers, friends, etc., and yet very little of it is of real value, for these people do not understand, at least most of them do not, avant-garde tendencies in modern literature. I would be so grateful to you if I could have some comment on my verse from you and your friends. The poems enclosed are truly representative ones.

I would like to mention that I have read several times, with great interest and admiration, your book, *The Overturned Lake*, and I believe it contains some of the very best Surreal poetry written in the United States. In the past I have read that great book, that has influenced me so much, *A Short Survey of Surrealism*, by David Gascoyne, Lemaître's *From Cubism to Surrealism in French Literature*, *Hölderlin's Madness*, *The Flowers of Evil* by Baudelaire, that wonderful manifesto that first inspired my ascent to paradise, *Several Have Lived* by Hugh Chisholm, and that very excellent section in the 1940 *New Directions*, "Values in Surrealism," and a host of other writings, on Surrealist art and literature including the very fine *Fantastic Art, Dada, Surrealism*, by Barr and Georges Hugnet.

In regard to the editorial in the current number of *View*, you state that other sides of the artistic question besides the unconscious must be considered. Does this mean that you have leanings away from Surrealism? Believe me, the poetry that is in your *Overturned Lake*, Hart Crane of the "Voyages," the South American Surrealists, Moro and Westphalen, and even my own work succeeds in renewing our deepest emotional contact with the world. Primitive art, through the untamed emotions, and Surrealism, through the world of dreams and desires, will be, after all is said and done, the only great artistic and literary movements of the twentieth century. Do they not renew this emotional contact that you speak of?

I am afraid I have taken up too much of your time. I would like to mention at this point, though, that I have been published only once, and that was in this year's *Anthology of California High School Poetry*, which is not much to shout about, though some would consider it quite an honor.

I hope that you can use one of my poems, and is there a chance that I can be included in the June issue of *View*? I suggest that you might give more attention to the poem of vertigo and madness, "The Ruins." If you can't use any of the poems in *View* please tell me of my chances for publication in, let's say *VVV*, *Accent*, or *The Chimera* or any other avant-garde magazine. I am enclosing a stamped self-addressed envelope for your convenience.

Thanking you very much,

Yours very truly,

Philip Lamantia

1943

SURREALISM IN 1943

San Francisco, October 8, 1943

Dear André Breton:

In your letter you have asked me to state my position on various matters of importance, mainly on Surrealism. Since you are aware that I am only fifteen years old, you must realize that my opinions on the issues I am to discuss here, will inevitably change to a certain extent. But I do not believe that these will be radical changes, since the basic content of the ideas I am now expressing and clinging to, I feel, will remain with me for some time to come.

First, I proclaim a formal adherence to Surrealism in its attitudes toward literature, art, society, and man, since it is of a purely revolutionary nature, which even before my knowledge of Surrealist theory, was part of my own individual temperament.

In the titanic effort of man to construct in the future a perfect or near-perfect society by using the full amount of his intellectual resources, man must think in terms of the "collectivity," not in terms of the "individual," also in terms of the collective want, not in terms of the individual want. Yet, even in this respect a balance between the two opposite poles must exist.

Surrealism is, I believe, fundamentally a philosophy endeavoring to form a unity between particular opposite forces at work in the world—the "unconscious" and the "conscious," the "collectivity" and the "individual," the "real" and the "unreal," the "poetic marvelous" and the "social." And because it is concerned with this "unity of opposites" it is based on Dialectical Materialism; also, in its literature and art, Surrealism carries this dialectic process to one of its farthest points. You have, of course, brilliantly analyzed much of this in the *Second Manifesto of Surrealism*.

At the present time when the forces of extreme principles are being felt almost by the whole world, a true revolutionary poet cannot help defying every appalling social and political instrument that has been the cause of death and exploitation in the capitalistic societies of the earth. If he is one for the transformation of the world, as he should be, and if he is not stupid, in relation to a method of approaching these vital issues, the poet will not be opposed to the Surrealist attitude.

Though I have not yet fully realized the implications of the external world, I nevertheless feel suited to express a revolt, and a contempt in my poetry or otherwise, for any system or form that stands for mechanistic thinking and the enslavement of man!

The synthesis of the two seemingly opposed "views," one of the conscious surface and the other of the interior world, that you speak of, I am confident will come when man has realized the greatness of his individuality and has become ready to use it for the good of the collectivity.

Those who are opposed to Surrealism in its attitude toward the external world are true reactionaries! And yet some of these same people begin borrowing from the literary and artistic forms used in Surrealism and endeavor to reconcile these methods with their own confused outlook, by claiming to "integrate" the artistic and literary elements into their own productions. In doing so, they take the roles of mimics, and to the public they present their performance under the guise of seeming originality.

To rebel! That is the immediate objective of poets! We cannot wait and will not be held back by those individuals, who are the prisoners of the bourgeoisie, and who have not the courage to go on fighting in the name of the "idea!" The "poetic marvelous" and the "unconscious" are the true inspirers of rebels and poets!

The voice of Lautréamont, pure, young, and feeding the fire that has begun to issue from my depths, is again heard proclaiming the immortal phrase, "Poetry should be made by all, not by one." These words must be realized in the future by the collectivity! The Surrealists have already done so!

With great admiration, I remain

Yours,

Philip Lamantia

THE TCHELITCHEW COVER

I still cannot find the correct adjective to describe my admiration for Tchelitchew's cover-painting. It is astounding beyond words; perhaps "marvelous" will do! Those tentacle-like objects coming from the eye are superb; the transparency in the painting is something I will never cease to admire.

1944

YOUNG POETS

Far more interesting than their poetry are the prefaces by four of the poets in this anthology: Eve Merriam, Jean Garrigue, Tennessee Williams, and John Frederick Nims. The verse is of hardly any consequence, and it adds nothing to the poetry of the new generation. These four poets are not promising, but already senile in their twenties.

Only the poetry of one of them: the Ecuadorian, Alejandro Carrión, seems important enough to deserve actual mention. (Significantly enough he offers no preface to his poems!) Carrión writes with a great deal of poetic ardor, and although he is not a clever technician, his automatic method of writing produces images and lines that mark him as a young, promising poet who will probably develop into a significant one.

Such lines as these show Carrión's fire, pure and simple, expressed in images that seem reflected in water:

> Come, behold the water invading the sleeping ships
> Come, hear the deaf murmur of the sunken temple
> Come, behold the flood which reaches the spirit.

At times, he seems to be altogether too facile, writing such obviously dull lines as these:

> But salvage Joy! Do not let Joy die!
> … Quickly! Save Joy!
> Do not let Joy die!

Usually Carrión does seem to be inspired, and his simplicity, which is not pretty or vulgar saving in spots, entails the use of an imagery automatic without being surrealist, and yet it cannot, because of its resemblance to Lorca, be considered completely derivative from Imagism.

The prefaces are interesting because they give a picture of what four so-called "promising young talents" think about poetry. They also give a picture of what poets should not think about poetry.

Eve Merriam's naive comments are mainly concerned with the resurrection of the antiquated argument between the so-called "Ivory Towerist" and the Whitmanesque type of poet who communicates his ideas in simple, "unpoetic" language. Why a poet appearing in a supposedly avant-garde collection should be concerned with this argument is a question to ask the editor and publisher. Miss Merriam's viewpoint in this argument is that she has tried to combine these two attitudes. With such lines as the following we can easily see how unsuccessful her theories, so far as her poetry is concerned, have been:

> Bestowing the silver coin like a discreet caress,
> the successful lover, passionate but wary;
> doting on her will-less, the spirit so deliciously unfree,
> his white dove, his doe, his innocent stupid fairy.
>
> (Title of the above: "The Business Man Tips His Favorite Waitress.")

Nims stupidly confesses that he understands neither poetry nor love. The rest of his preface is simply an apology for this obviously affected and hypocritically modest statement. He states also that "the human situation" is of greater interest to him than poetry. This denotes his failure as a poet and artist. The poet, unlike the rest of mankind today, identifies, in the literal sense, his inner-self (from which all poetry springs) with the external world ("the human situation" as Nims terms it). It is this identification, which is made possible through love, that makes the poet unique. Man, in the modern world, definitely splits himself in halves, living in reality and in the spirit, without realizing the relationship between these two realms. To say that "In a universe of ganglion and nebula, of intellectual and ethical dimensions yet more impressive, poetry is perhaps a trivial thing..." is obviously a sign that Nims is not a poet with any strong convictions. His attitude is symbolic of the confused and weak academician who does not understand the great power poetry will wield in the future, because he is involved with an approach and technique which reduce poetry to the classroom where it is treated as a mere insignificant supplement to the other subjects being taught. That is, poetry is not thought of as being in the world, and the world is never thought of as being in poetry.

Jean Garrigue's preface is much more intelligent. But it contributes little or nothing to one's knowledge of poetry, restating, as it does, all the most obvious principles of the poet's vision of life. Garrigue could have made his preface into one paragraph instead of two and a half pages. And yet he seems not to be very sure about what he is saying. His whole analysis is fragmentary, too much a parody of antiquated ideas which today hold little water unless they are supported by other ideas which contribute to a more expansive view on "the poet's business," as Garrigue puts it.

Tennessee Williams writes two prefaces to his poems: titling one "Frivolous Version" and the other "Serious Version." To begin with, I think the "frivolous" preface should have been titled "Serious Version" and vice-versa. He poses the most inane questions imaginable, asking poets "how they live" and "how they get along." He then tells us how he won prizes for poetry in high school, how he wrote poetry behind his employer's back, and how he knew poets in New Orleans, Los Angeles, St. Louis, and Chicago. His naiveté is insupportable, and one begins to feel that he should have kept on winning prizes at school, should not have written poetry on his job, and should not have met provincial poets who inspired him to go on writing despite his obvious lack of talent.

1945

AN AMERICAN OPINION

It interested me to see what you would say on the atomic bomb; your position is, of course, a valid one. It is impossible to believe that the Allied governments will ever use the sources of atomic energy other than for destructive purposes, except in certain industries where the capitalists could profit from its constructive use. Only a few days ago I read in the papers that the chairman on the Congressional board for the "control" of atomic energy (an American General) made the statement that conditions in "civilian" life are so "complicated" that *decades* would pass before this great source of energy could be used extensively by civilians. Decades, my eye! He means that it *never* will be used if the government can help it.

The atomic bomb, to me, is the symbol of the de-humanized, moral irresponsibility that so characterizes Western European and American civilization at the present time. The insensibility of the American press towards the Hiroshima A-Bomb raid is a good example. Not one American newspaper, liberal or otherwise, seemed in the least shocked over the fact that literally hundreds of thousands died by the effect of one bomb, not one line of sympathy for these people (who were enemies only in the strict military sense); in short, a thorough disregard for human values. As Dwight Macdonald pointed out in *Politics*, this complete lack of humanity is, for the most part, a recent manifestation and did not exist let's say when the Spanish War was on. This de-humanization which now prevails (which came to its height in Fascist countries) began to sweep the world some thirty years ago and since that time has eaten away, like a cancer, the love-impulse among people. The principles of hate, aggression, torture, and the will-to-war have become so powerful in the mass-psychology of the world, that they have almost annihilated the principles of love and freedom. The atomic bomb is the outward expression of this basic psychological malady. Totalitarianism is its political expression; American democracy reveals the moral irresponsibility that springs from it. The revolutionary of our times—and I do not mean just politically, for that is not enough—to have any sort of valid position must attach himself to a philosophy of love; politically and socially Anarchism, if correctly interpreted, offers this. A very interesting book by a one-time disciple of Freud, Wilhelm Reich, treats with these problems in a very objective manner. Dr. Reich was thrown out of the Psycho-analytical society about fifteen years ago because he dared to bring to light the relationship between the political, moral, and social patterns in our society and their detrimental effects upon the individual's psychic life and in turn its effects upon these patterns. The book was recently translated into English under the title *Function of the Orgasm*, and though it has not as yet gained wide recognition, in advanced circles, it is one of the most revolutionary books of our time.

As a poet I can envision no other position of moral responsibility to myself and to others than a consistently revolutionary individualism—something that can only come in its own in the world, if Anarchism were established in the hearts of men.

1945

CONSCIENTIOUS OBJECTOR'S STATEMENT

December 3, 1945

Selective Service Hdqrs.
Local Board No. 79
513 Valencia Street
San Francisco 10, Calif.

To Whom It May Concern:

In order to clarify and extend my answers in the Form for Conscientious Objector, I am submitting the following statement which I hope will give you a more precise knowledge of my position and attitude.

For centuries the imperfection of man has concerned theologians, philosophers, and poets. This problem is a complex one, but in our time it has become noticeable that this so-called imperfection arose from certain deep-rooted principles which govern a great deal of man's nature—all contrary to the love-impulse and principle, which has always been the well-spring of creativity and happiness. If I were to analyze these principles of imperfection I would name them as such: hate, force, aggression, torture, and finally the culmination point for all four: mass murder, War. These principles are those of destruction, and in times of war they become its instrument. To answer how or why these destructive principles became so much a part of man's nature is extremely difficult when attempted from a purely materialistic interpretation, as one would finally be forced to consider the essence of the question still veiled in mystery. What I understand as the Original Sin—and I am not alone in this non-materialist interpretation—is the "dawn of consciousness," the faculty of the intellect asserting itself over man's primal nature, in which a harmony existed between body and spirit, causing an inter-relationship of the two. The Serpent tempted Eve to eat of the "tree of knowledge," adding that she and Adam would thereby become gods. Not content with the things of the spirit and the body, not content with pure feelings of love, man Fell and became a slave to his intellect, the well of conflicts, the absence of peace. From then on he was forced to make choices, to form intellectual judgments, to progress toward purely material perfection through his intellect. I assert that from the intellect man derives his imperfection, his hate, his will to coerce others, to torture and to make war. It is not through the intellect that an individual becomes free, but through a spiritual understanding of the purpose of life, which arises from a physical, non-intellectual communion with the world. In the words of the seventeenth century Christian mystic, Thomas Traherne: "You never enjoy the world aright till the sea itself floweth in your veins, till you are clothed with the heavens and crowned with the stars," or as D.H. Lawrence said only a few years ago: "For man, the vast marvel is to be alive ... a part of the living incarnate cosmos. I am a part of the sun as my eye is part of me. That I am a part of the earth my feet know perfectly and my blood is a part of the sea ..."

The XIX century dream of man's final perfection through scientific progress has become, at least theoretically, realized with the control of atomic energy. But under what circumstances did this come about? In a war. And how did it manifest itself? In the form of the most monstrous weapon of all time: The Atomic Bomb. The atomic bomb becomes the symbol of man's destructive principles brought to their final stage of development. It is to this state of affairs that the whole materialist-progressive tradition of our civilization has brought us. This tradition, which is the dominating one in our time, is a product of the Original Sin existing in men. It is only those, who in the spirit of Christ, strive in the opposite direction from this disease in the souls of men, that find peace and purpose in their lives. Not only have Christian and other religious writers in our time, such as T. S. Eliot, Berdyaev, and D. H. Lawrence, become aware of this basic malady, but also prominent psychologists—in particular Wilhelm Reich, whose analysis of the distortion of the love-impulse, among men, proves on a mere objective plane of investigation, what was intuited by the writers of Genesis. It has become increasingly clear in the contemporary world that one of the greatest of evils stems from the inability for man to "love his neighbor as he loves himself." But I also affirm that men have ceased to regard their object of love—in the final, universal sense—they have lost their spiritual life. The object of love, when man turns within himself, is God. When this love is directed outwardly, through a particular human vehicle, and having been a product of a profound communication with Life, the emanation is so powerful that no evil can invade the individual. Love must be complete or not at all. To use force to abolish an evil is sheer hypocrisy; what is left is a lesser-evil born out of the first. But not only will the evil remain, outwardly, but within the person. I am reminded of Simone Weil (a Christian political writer who died a few years ago) and her brilliant essay on "The Iliad, or the Poem of Force," wherein she says: "To define force—it is that 'x' that turns anybody who is subjected to it into a 'thing.' Exercised to the limit, it turns man into a thing in the most literal sense: it makes a corpse out of him." It is this purge of the spirit which takes place whenever an individual uses force, whether in war or in everyday life. It is in war that man loses any spiritual value and becomes a mere instrument in the hands of force, of every principle and idea that is contrary to Love.

* * * * * * * * * * *

As an individualist, I intend to be quite free from what I consider any social evil—namely the State. I think it possible for an individual to contribute very little, even if asked or forced to, or nothing at all, to the workings of the State, or for that matter, to the progress of civilization in general—and still live in the midst of it. Therefore I certainly refuse to directly participate in, or be at the mercy of, that part of the State which comprises its greatest evil: the military. Any participation in military "life" would eventually lead to the subjection to those principles of force, hate, aggression, conflict, and destruction of human lives which I have spoken of. Not only do I refuse, because of my convictions, to involve myself in using these principles against others, but I refuse to have the coercive techniques of militarism turned against me. I do not believe in the worldly authority of any aspect of this civilization or society. I believe in the inner authority that lies at the base of my religious and moral convictions, and that it will be my only guide. A complete submission to any worldly authority, demanding participation in war or its aftermath, would be an unpardonable sin against the essence of life, which is Love, and *not* destruction.

Though, in a sense, the Second World War has ended, I still object to participate in any service which is under military authority, and directed towards the occupation of this or that nation. I consider the so-called "peace" that follows a war to be as evil, if not more evil, than the war itself—for therein are sown the seeds of the next one. Anyone with the slightest knowledge of world affairs can see that this is the situation at the present time. But even if another "world war" were not inevitable, I still would refuse to have any direct concern with the aftermath of the last, for it still would reduce me to the state of an instrument directed towards these ends, destructive at their base, which the majority of men and nations accept and live by. Finally it must be said that everything returns to the "I," that I stand apart from the general stream, if I wish to, by reacting, physically and spiritually, to the world, and to myself, in terms of my bodily-spiritual convictions—and that essentially my individualistic conception of life is entirely valid, buttressed, as it is, by certain Christian ethical concepts and by a traditional, yet intensely personal, sense of moral responsibility.

I hope that this statement, together with my Conscientious Objector's Form, will be sufficient evidence to prove my sincerity in the matter, and that my exemption from military service will be granted.

LETTER FROM SAN FRANCISCO

San Francisco and Northern California have recently become busy centers of intellectual and creative activity, differing radically from general American trends of the thirties. A generation is rising that is remarkably alive to new orientations—new methods of expression, new moral and intellectual concerns. It is largely a post-war generation; the pre-war Pacific coast was, putting it mildly, a cultural desert. Many of the new writers and artists came with the general influx of Easterners and Middle-westerners during the war; some were conscientious objectors who had been sent to concentration camps in the west; and some were people who found they could work here far better than in wartime New York.

It is still too early to catalogue all this turbulent activity, but I should say that the prevailing direction is towards anarchism and varieties of religious personalism. By and large, the attitude is similar to that for which *Now*, *Poetry London*, *Poetry Quarterly*, and *Transformation* are spokesmen in England. Here, as in England, it is an attitude born of disgust with the bankruptcy of pre-war radical intellectuals who tended to statism in one form or another. The new people flatly reject those who, in the thirties, were voicing their indignation at capitalism and the State in the pages of *Parti-

san Review, and who were not at all reluctant about selling themselves to the Office of War Information or simply keeping their mouths shut for the duration. The popularity of Henry Miller, a wartime arrival here, rests largely on his inspiring denunciations of the war, of his protest against the mass use of human lives to perpetuate a diseased society. Who, among the pillars of *Partisan Review*, turned "defender of the Four Freedoms," could have been capable of writing *Murder the Murderer* which in the simplest terms said the same thing most radicals had said five or ten years before!

One of the few poets here whose reputation was established before the war is Kenneth Rexroth, long a resident of San Francisco, an advocate of pacifist-anarchism for many years. Excerpts from his two books of poems (*In What Hour* and *The Phoenix and the Tortoise*) have recently appeared in several English magazines. Rexroth extended the boundaries of objectivism and intentionally emphasized the anti-theoretical image to develop a moving, highly personalized poetry. His long philosophical poem, *The Phoenix and the Tortoise*, is excellent for its erudition and metrical structure, and for its vision of the tragic interplay of individual and society; both tone and thought are at once religious and revolutionary.

Of the younger poets, William Everson, born in California, is notable for a unique earthiness and direct honesty rarely found in the thick literary quarterlies run by university-bred intellectuals. He has written and printed on his own press several booklets. His best work to date is that written in a Civilian Public Service Camp for conscientious objectors. These poems (*War Elegies* and *Waldport Poems*) are intensely experiential and deal, as Everson has said, with "a kind of life that has become almost universal: the life of the camp, the life of enforced confinement, individual repression, sexual segregation," the life of millions who, by the nature of our society, were, and still are being, forced into conscription, concentration, labor, and prison camps. His poetry has been praised highly in many quarters, and soon a collected edition is being brought out by New Directions.

In most cases the poetry being written out here seems to differ considerably from the usual thing one sees nowadays. There is a tendency to write simply, to say what is important only, that which deals with love, death and the personal experience. Most of it reflects, less and less, the experimentalism of the twenties and early thirties. There is Robert Duncan, author of the recent *Heavenly City, Earthly City*, a rather incantatory kind of poetry, very impassioned and stylistically, akin to Milton and Surrey. Thomas Parkinson, who acknowledges affinities with Crabbe and Cowper, writes some very moving, personal poetry. Richard Moore's elegiac and pastoral poems have a quiet, almost restrained, quality about them, influenced, largely, by Chinese poetry. Sanders Russell writes what he calls a "poetry of mental images," of a quietist, closely Oriental turn of mind. Another young poet who as yet has not published widely, is Robert Stock, attempting a personalization of a mystical-religious tradition in esoteric Christianity. Also notable is Janet Lewis, author of the recent *Bravery of Earth*, for many years a writer of well-balanced lyrical poetry in a modern, yet traditional, vein. Of the younger generation, we have a very promising talent displayed in the work of Patricia Umsted who has recently appeared in the little magazines. There are others, of course, young poets in their twenties of varying degrees of talent, of whom it is perhaps not necessary to speak at the moment. What I am getting at with these brief sidelights (which in themselves may not prove very important) is that there seems to be less interest in foreign importations than was the case with the writers who appeared between the pages of *transition*. The influence of symbolism, of the baroque, or, for that matter, of surrealism, is not as apparent as before, though it most certainly does continue to be assimilated in the poetry. The tendency is away from the over-rhetorical so popular a decade ago with imitators of Hart Crane.

Most of the local writers I mentioned above, including C.O.'s, painters, and other intellectuals, gathered together in an anarchist discussion group which held weekly meetings, in San Francisco, with the purpose of clarifying and re-evaluating libertarian thought. In the past, San Francisco had been quite a center for anarchism. Emma Goldman and Alexander Berkman were here in the years before World War I, publishing their magazine, *The Bomb*. Bakunin, himself, was here in the last century, California being the last outpost of the Black International. In the hey-day of Stalinism there remained only small social groups cut off from the major political and intellectual stream. But slowly, and with the general discrediting of traditional socialist radicals, most young intellectuals have come to an entirely different point of view than what was represented by the major radical tendencies of the immediate past. Around here there has developed a non-doctrinaire anarchism, thoroughly lacking in the illusions of nineteenth-century thought; in short, a moral criticism of existing society. It is influenced by the dynamic vitalism of D. H. Lawrence, the Lawrence of *The Fantasia of the Unconscious* and *The Plumed Serpent*; by such works as Berdyaev's *Destiny of Man* and *Slavery and Freedom* that set forth a revolutionary Christian personalism, basically consistent with the orthodox tenets of anarchism; and by Albert Schweitzer whose interpretation of values, in *The*

Decay and Restoration of Civilization, is an undeniable contribution. Living in a world of progressive inhumanity, at the tail-end of Western civilization, those who reject society have come to assume that the main validity of anarchism lies in terms of the individual's moral and social opposition: it is a philosophy of life for those who intend to keep themselves as clean as possible and who are ready to meet any drastic invasion of the State with a resistance of the whole personality.

Out of these meetings, there came the impetus towards the creation of a magazine. Entitled *The Ark*, it was planned as a gathering point for writers and artists dedicated to independent and non-statist positions. The first issue is appearing shortly with the inclusion of several English writers—Alex Comfort, George Woodcock, and D. S. Savage, as well as such Americans as Paul Goodman, E. E. Cummings, Kenneth Patchen, etc. Also, as I am writing this, I am informed of a proposed international journal of ethics and philosophy Mr. Rexroth is to edit. Proceeding from a libertarian basis, it will endeavour to include work by Berdyaev, Martin Buber, Suzuki, Roger Caillois, Camus, etc.

Independent of any movement is *Circle*, edited from Berkeley by the poet George Leite. It has pursued for nine issues a policy of publishing avant-garde literature and art from all corners of the world, as well as being an outlet for those living in this area. Leite is also the inaugurator of *Circle Editions*, which have recently brought out books by Lawrence Durrell, *Zero*, and *The Black Book*, and Albert Cossery's *Men God Forgot*. Also being published from Berkeley is *Contour*, the first number appearing currently. In the past, the publisher of New Directions, James Laughlin, has given space to several California writers and is planning currently a little anthology of their poetry for the next *Annual*. Another publisher, Bern Porter, is continuing in the same direction, already having brought out books by several young poets around here, including Robert Duncan, Leonard Wolfe (*Hamadryad Hunted*), and myself (*Erotic Poems*).

That the influence of the various currents I have described is growing, can be evidenced by the numerous activities the San Francisco Bay Area has recently witnessed, ranging from poetry readings to the openings of new galleries and the public showings of avant-garde movies. And, in the midst of all this, a certain note of notoriety was struck by the appearance in a national monthly magazine, of wide circulation, *Harper's* for April 1947, of a sneering, in fact libellous article by a personality described best by the word "stalinoid." Entitled "The New Cult of Sex and Anarchy," it presented a very falsified picture of the general scene. Besides getting all mixed up about who represented what, the author accuses everyone with an anarchist position as being a follower of Wilhelm Reich's sometimes dubious psychology of orgastic potency. It is true that in many intellectual circles here, as elsewhere, Reich's analysis of sexual disorganization in modern society, resulting from—and developing out of—the interplay of recent social and political currents, has attracted quite a response and, in some, an adherence. But in spite of the basic truthfulness of his findings, I know of few who have taken his word as the final one or who view his theories of biophysics with much approval. The *Harper's* article also went on to further misrepresentations that have finally prompted largely the recent editorial drive the Hearst papers, through the efforts of the *San Francisco Examiner*, directed against Henry Miller, particularly, and the influence of anarchism, generally. Miller, who is not really affiliated with anarchism, has been living in the Big Sur redwood country south of San Francisco for several years. It is easy to be too critical of Miller's writings. He probably is not as great as his admirers would have one believe. It is also true that he mixes up Vivekananda and astrological readings with what is otherwise serious, well-directed writing. By what Miller says, and through his fabulous efforts to get heard, he has emerged as a force of no small importance. He has consistently denounced what needs to be denounced. His protest is designed, primarily, for the unsophisticated who may find him as the only voice audible, and through him be led to the sounder values of others in the past who have said the same things. Miller's world-view is that of an angry, yet humble, individual who refuses to make peace with a society in which inequality and brutality have probably degraded the human personality to a point never before witnessed in history. His cry is the death cry, to be sure; to some it may also be an expression of the coming of spring.

Attacking Miller as a "philosopher of hate and doom," the articles against him have culminated in a Hearst drive to oust him and his influence from the Big Sur country. Again, the old stupidity and bigotry of America are at work, and may easily culminate in violence; such a move, even if it does not lead to open violence by the defenders of the status quo, is a reminder, to all those who may have forgotten, that unless a writer toes the line, or keeps quiet, he remains an implacable enemy of an order of things whose God is Mammon and a nation now living off the blood of war and the spiritual, economic and social disorganization of the rest of the world.

1947

EDITORIAL FROM THE ARK (1947)

BY PHILIP LAMANTIA,

SANDERS RUSSELL,

AND ROBERT STOCK

In direct opposition to the debasement of human values made flauntingly evident by the war, there is rising among writers in America, as elsewhere, a social consciousness which recognizes the integrity of the personality as the most substantial and considerable of values. However, this recognition is still restricted to either small groups or to isolated individuals, and has few adequate organs for expression. Among these two only, *Retort* and England's *Now*, are of a literary nature. The others—*Freedom, Why?, Politics*, and *The Catholic Worker*—are periodicals of a purely political intent.

Present day society, which is becoming more and more subject to the State with its many forms of corrupt power and oppression, has become the real enemy of individual liberty. Because mutual aid and trust have been coldly, scientifically destroyed; because love, the well of being, has been methodically parched; because fear and greed have become the prime ethical movers, States and State-controlled societies continue to exist. Only the individual can cut himself free from this public evil. He can sever the forced relations between himself and the State, refuse to vote or go to war, refuse to accept the moral irresponsibility yoked onto him. Today, at this catastrophic point in time, the validity if not the future of the anarchist position is more than ever established. It has become a polished mirror in which the falsehoods of political modes stand naked. No honest person, if he has looked into this mirror, can morally support a government of any description, whether it be a State-capitalist Soviet Union, a capitalist America, a fascist Spain, or any considered society wherein an idea is woven into a blanket of law and cast over a living people from above. Any inorganic thing made authority over the organic is morally weakening and makes annihilating warfare inevitable.

Every small good a government performs is outweighed by a very real and really appalling evil. People who have had no experience in these matters tend to minimize the brutality of the police, judiciary prejudice, the abuses of the polls, and the failure of the law to protect those in need of protection: on one hand those who exist in conditions of misery and neglect in State prisons, asylums, and homes, and on the other the depressed groups who in their daily lives are subject to the forces of hatred and ignorance.

Therefore, we are concerned with a thorough revaluation of the relations between the individual and society. We hope that such a revaluation will stimulate thought and action. It is with this hope that we are issuing *The Ark*, a magazine with consistent anti-statist attitudes. We shall seek to present the various aspects of libertarian thought, of a religious, personal, or political nature, and shall examine ideas of the past and their relation to recent developments in social and political thinking.

We believe that social transformation must be the aim of any revolutionary viewpoint, but we recognize the organic, spontaneous revolt of individuals as presupposing such a transformation. The vanguard of such a revolt is becoming a potent force in contemporary literature. Certain older writers who have preserved clarity of outlook toward the existing false political and social values will here be seen in a new perspective; young writers who suffer lack of recognition will have a forum for their work.

1947

CONSCIENTIOUS OBJECTOR'S STATEMENT II

Jan 5 1949
Selective Service
Local Board #47
2199 Bancroft Way
Berkeley 4, Calif.

To Whom It May Concern:

   Space not permitting on the form, the following is in answer to questions 1 and 2 of Series II:

* * * * *

I believe in a supreme being which I understand to be the source of all human potential; the ultimate of existence and of which manifestations, apparent in the temporal world, point to certain known directions of human behavior and endeavor. If I am aware of a responsibility in relation to what, for the sake of mutual understanding, I call God (which I read also as Reality) I am nevertheless equally responsible to what is of God's essence in the temporal universe: namely all other beings and my relations to them. Of the manifestations of this existential reality, i.e. God, creation and the creative act are, above all, the very beginning and end, and it is on the side of continual creativity that man works toward either salvation or damnation. Destruction, therefore, I understand as only valid, in the eyes of God, insofar that it clearly foreshadows, indeed holds within its limits, the active creative germ. It is my firm conviction, already expressed in the last war in which my claim for exemption was finally upheld, that war and militarism, which exists ultimately for war, are the most blatant violation of the creative principle in the universe. Destruction, organized destruction of the bodies and souls of men is the explicit principle of every known army in the world. Furthermore this harnessing of destructive forces, by man, is the peculiar work of man, though he has always, irresponsibly, invoked, in its varying aspects, the spirit of God to aid him in his act of undoing. It is upon this essential principle of creativity, of what is of ultimate value in man, that my claim for exemption from military service rests—for it is exactly this capacity for active creativity that makes of man a personality distinguished from a mere object in the midst of a shattering universe. But it is the intention, implicit or explicit, of all coercive institutions, of which the military is the example par excellence, to make of a man a mere "thing" and, paraphrasing what someone else recently wrote on this problem, of turning man into a "thing" in the most literal sense: making a corpse of him; this the end product of harnessed destructive activity, typified, so blatantly, by atomic warfare and all the other extreme techniques of modern mass murder.

Simply stated then, I am thoroughly opposed to those ends to which any military organization is dedicated, for the moral-spiritual reasons mentioned above and because of a very deep centered individuality, i.e., my ahistorical position in present-day society, through which I am always aware of the great dividing line between my most essential creative activity, as a poet, and the opposing tide of energy coming from almost every other far-reaching endeavor carried out about me. For today, the nature of society has brought about a condition of being in which man views himself, if he so wishes, as an individual cut off from the official institutions and historic phases of the society in which he lives; indeed, in my own case, there is no question that I neither wish to ally nor participate with any of the known political, social, or economic struggles—wars, is a better term—going on somewhere where I am not, nor wish to be. How strange it seems, then, to me that I should have anything directly to do with such an unreal institution as the army, or, for that matter, with this selective service board!

Sincerely,

Philip Lamantia

TWO INTRODUCTIONS TO JOHN HOFFMAN

Untitled Introduction to *Journey to the End*

The true, the magical, the highly qualified poet—it must be said: the born poet—it can never be too strongly emphasized, is a being whose work speaks most clearly for itself. And so it is that I write this introduction primarily to praise and reveal John Hoffman who, dead at 24, lives in these finely conceived poems that create a universe of words and music whose meaning and purpose extends directly in and from the context of his poetry.

    At my first meeting with him in 1947 (in San Francisco, where he was born in 1928) he showed me poems, subsequently lost or destroyed,* that were the unmistakable signs of a rare Appearance, and indicated a freedom sought beyond the confines of fetid derivation exemplified blatantly in the literary scene, and so deadly for the poet who, by his nature, is an instigator of all forms of transcendence. John Hoffman's poetry is the authentic instance: by precise artistry, by pure intention, it extends out of what he knew to be essential in the self. And this integrity and bird-like departure devel-

*LAMANTIA'S NOTE: To my knowledge there may be in existence a manuscript of poems, perhaps in a green manila folder, written before 1950 and which Hoffman mentioned leaving with an unnamed friend in

New York City. It is hoped that through this present publication this, or any other mss of his, will come to light. Anyone having such information is asked to communicate with me care of the publisher.

oped with greater power, by many completions of flight, in the last two years before his death. (These *last* poems are those he has titled; the untitled ones are earlier, written sometime before 1949.) Though he refrained from magazine publication, he did contemplate seeing his poems in book form, and it is a credit to Bern Porter that this poetry does not have to continue circulating in manuscript only, among a small circle of friends.

Eloquently simple, but nonetheless extensive, are these exfoliations from a highly charged brevity in which the poet makes those magical connections between the inner and the outer vision, between mind and wind, eyes and sun, sea and sand, creating an allegory of the self whose wonder is motion: above all, a movement towards death prophetically crystallized in several poems. John Hoffman is inspired from the profound limits where the soul discovers, and is created by, a magnetism of symbols and imagery; he is able to draw forth a world, a new dimension of being, and make heard a music sometimes angular, sometimes sharp, sometimes glowing, distinct and clean. This is the excellence that cannot be taught but, by necessity and inner learning, emerges lucid and strong from that *source* the poet, in the exceptional sense, alone and by persistent desire to *see*, has the capacity to invoke. This penetration and invocation is more than a mere act of will: it is a *process* in which he is continually involved, up to and after the making of poems. It is the only absolute involvement for the poet and demands everything from him. More than the outer coverings, it demands the core of nerves, brain and blood, toward an attainment *more-than-life*—a spending of powers to renew power. And it is this process that I find in the secret marrow of John Hoffman's poems and by which I claim for him a place and an efficacy—it almost goes without saying—the world denied him.

More than ever, the world in its super-smugness, by its hatred of poetry and by specialized varieties of obscurantism (perpetuated and created in the microcosmic realm of the arts), paralyzed by the usurping powers of mediocrity, high and low, and with the greatest fear of transcendence—forbids, absolutely, any total, direct manifestation of poetic power. Blinded by hostility and ignorance, the world—social, literary-artistic—does not allow a space for poetry when it appears, except in those cases of subtle appropriation in which poets, *other than for reasons of poetry*, are transformed into mouthpieces of an era or are made to serve as masters of a tendency categorized for critical seminars.

It is precisely through this misuse of poetry conducted by a band of arbitrary, droning critics, that poetry continues to be fettered to the page and is isolated in academies. Therefore the poet, under pressure of organized denial and suffocation—a dispellation of atomized and atomizing sickness—is forbidden to begin on the highest terms (i.e., at each stage by the poet himself who alone knows the ultimate reason for his being) that concrete, objectified, unfettered *realization in space* for which a true poem is an authentic symbolical sign. For the poet appears unknown, deprived and shunted, in the midst of a confused, organized ignorance paying the slightest lip-service to the formation of a living culture. And a living culture can begin only when poetry emerges, full-bodied from this hateful isolation, with all its exultation and stabilizing power, a regenerative and equilibrious power for which it is the purest representation in the face of all sick civilizations. As John Hoffman said: in that *"time of birds beginnings"* ... by *"apocalyptics unanimous"* ... who now *"disengage and deburrow."*

The prose poems evoke for me a glyph of John Hoffman's personal history, and I will permit myself to speak of what all of us who knew him, the few who were his friends, may remember as remarkable in his presence: a pervading sense of intactness, a quiet, effusive gaiety contained by a certain solemnity and unequalled grace ... above all: the unpretentious offering of his whole being turned to the far limits from which he returned bearing, intact, the fruits of his vision. The external circumstances of his life—in the five years I knew him—were nothing but "marginal." Denied economic security, holding down odd jobs for brief periods, and, once, equipped with a copy of Lautréamont's *Maldoror*, he embarked as a sailor out of New York, visiting Rio de Janeiro and Montevideo, Lautréamont's birthplace. He had the wanderlust, and after peregrinating to the central parts of Mexico (he died in Guadalajara in January 1952), he wrote me of a desire to go further south, "build a raft and make it to Ecuador"; he was fated to make it to the Sun.

Mexico D.F., October, 1954.

The Legend in Praise of John Hoffman

John Hoffman's poems surprised me when I read them the night I met him in a North Beach cafe in 1948 in San Francisco. None of that group is in this book (John probably lost them), though they are similar to what follows. He had read my *Erotic Poems* as well as having imbibed as a youth in his father's library Rimbaud, Lautréamont, the memoirs of a physician, etc. His look was often like the gaze of, his whole countenance resembled, Dali's imaginary portrait of Isidore Ducasse.

After his death a manuscript was collected from among his "effects." His being stricken down by paralysis, in Puerto Vallarta, Mexico, 1952, and subsequent death in a hospital in Guadalajara are all I know together with the fact that a certificate, in Spanish, mentions cremation ... In his death, John is alive. For he made many of these poems knowing he would go out before his twenty-fifth year. VIDE: *Death*, "prophesied balloon." This is epiphanical poetry surviving the bombast and noise of Madison Ave Beat and post-beat. In the early fifties, in New York, I saw John on the scene with Gerd Stern, Sheri Martinelli, Harry Honig, Christopher Maclaine, Iris Brody, Carl Solomon, Allen Ginsberg, and Jack Kerouac. Here are poems of silent tundra, dunes of interior real stillness—underwater explosions!—Here's the lyric Hoffman. Trouvere, singing a girl's arc and grace, the nostalgia of deserted streets, swamps, jungles, and cities of the imagination as John walked poor and alone through New York, New Orleans, San Francisco, Rio, Montevideo. Once I received a postcard from South America where he wore a copy of *Chants de Maldoror* stuck in a pocket of his blue jeans.

This poetry demands the ear and eyes of intelligence. It covers the interior scene of what is happening outside. It nails you, this poetry, to the Absolute, to the splendid images of sea, sun, and sand, turning you onto the eye, the Third Eye, revolving spiral to the sun in the Heavens and the dark one inside you.

Read them perhaps a hundred times, these absolute poems and you shall see they still swing, they change and expand, these soft diamonds of John, scribe of the Albatross, whose mysterious, high presence, deep in them, is communicated, released for flight when the right metempsychotic response is made (in the now and ancient sense of the "communication from spirit to spirit"). John Hoffman is heir to the family of Poe, Melville, Samuel Greenberg, and Hart Crane ... Listen ... O wild, beatific, mad ones everywhere ... for the Angels who sent their thoughts to John are among us ready to touch off the coming of the Inca Kings.

Farewell Final Albatross is the title John Hoffman gave this book I have been honored to introduce and he is reading in Heaven.

February 27, 1959

HYMNS TO ST. GERYON (1959) BY MICHAEL MCCLURE

It will crowd *you* out of your lives—*his* "SHOULDER," that is! That's McClure, you see!—if you have visionary eyes you'll know what *that* "shoulder" means! McClure's poems can bring on dangerous motor responses—believe me, I'm not fooling!!!

Read Michael McClure's new book, *Hymns to St. Geryon*—because it's tough, turgid, tongue tied, tremulous, triumphant formless, and full of BODY!

A *passage* to a people of erotic dreams, thrusts and voids, a book inspired by a man's overwhelming self love, self knowledge and selflessness, the flems and flames of nerves, grindings, pressures,—breakthroughs—the very rhythm of no rhythms—not another *pose*, but STANCE, history according to his inner, third and bursting EYE. Here's a poet who is also A GREAT CONTEMPORARY PAINTER!!! an abstract expressionist, action painter in words.

BIOGRAPHICAL NOTE IN <u>THE NEW AMERICAN POETRY, 1945-1960</u>

Born 1927 in San Francisco. Lived in New York City, Mexico, Europe, and North Africa. Hailed by André Breton as an authentic surrealist poet; first appearances in *View*, 1943–45; broke with surrealism by 1946. Since then mostly underground, and traveling.

VISION AND INSTIGATION
OF MESCALINE 1961

TO ERNESTO CARDENAL

The omens were favorable   banners would blow sonic views of sacred gold
may the Visitation come from motions of lapis lazuli thru the wind
Ornette blows slow shuffle ramble blues
may the Visitation come THRU that I build the city in holy letters—city in
   this world formed from meditations of poets -mandala/city radiant from
   burning waters of said Potomic—

all at once! USA TURNED ON TO MESCALINE! God Who is Poetry Poetry
   Who is God IMMEDIATE EXPERIENCE OF THE CONTEMPLATIVE VI-
   SION revealing God in all things Mescaline is brain food

USA is starved for chemical/vegetable visionary experience—deadly alcohol preferred to benign wide/awake visionary transcendental bliss producing mystically impulsed drugs—
                    Mescaline can help to cure alcoholism,

heroin addiction—natural means to see God! MESCALINE NOW LONGEST/LASTING MOST INTENSE READILY AVAILABLE NON-ADDICTIVE VESSEL OF TRANSCENDENT VISION! MESCALINE IS VISION PRODUCING ALKALOIDS OUT OF PEYOTE ANCIENT INDIAN SACRAMENTAL PLANT NATIVE TO RIO GRANDE OF USA AND MEXICO! A REAL HOLY AMERICAN DRUG!

If Mescaline becomes generally available in USA we shall learn to love choose to love—individual love for all things—love for oneself—love for the proximate person—love for all proximate persons—
Thru the Drug the ancient fundamental vision of Christ is immediately sensually perceptible to those open to the SPIRIT. The Drug is the contempo-

rary way forward to the rediscovery of God IN CONSCIOUSNESS—in each individual consciousness in the collective consciousness of USA and thru this consciousness, redirection of energy towards a new society in revolution founded ultimately on universal principles of transcendent Reality—

Mescaline is a natural "grace" in imitation of supernatural Grace, the beginning of the Beatific Vision HERE AND NOW. Heaven is perceptible, now, thru Mescaline. Mescaline, taken generally, shall move and open conscious life to rediscovery of highest religious truth—a necessary bio/chemic impulse to erection of spiritual order thru all orbits of social life. The only person who may not "need" Mescaline is the fully integrated holy contemplative who each moment experiences contemplation and is an active/contemplative *and* perfect saint.

THE BEAT GENERATION

AUGUST 30, 1961

I've been asked to write bout the beat generation, poetry in the U.S., and I finally came to remember what seems to be the secret of my generation, called: beat, hip, cool—have it in parts, even!—to beatific generation but, actually now, "apocalyptic" generation, the generation that came awake, into "awareness," the keystone of Hip, in its origins, inside and at the end of World War II with the advent of the Bomb—and this is what I think and others have thought parallel to—We were so frantic to *live* in certitude of sudden death that we laid, like pale kings and queens, our hands on all that was around us—to MAKE IT!!! "IT" meaning anything that was not identifiable with the stupid, synthetic half/life of postAtomicBomb man, his exploded cities, literature, art, his corny mis/education, his phantom governments, his *corny* reasoning, sick politics, his stand/in over/organized religions, U.S. man's Sell, the silly "soft sell," his insanity/producing "hard sell"—the end of civilization—kept going another few years by fact of its integral destruction sustained, actually, by the Bomb and therefore obsolete social/economic forms, obsolete by fact of the great Change apparently few could understand but which more and more now understand and will come to understand as the possibility of New Forms, a new leavening of the Earth takes place, as man learns to feed himself without hate and ignorance, anger and stupidity, misdirection and fraud, in order to evolve to that point when he will seek more than bread in quest of his Divine Destination!

A few poets of my generation tried to live in voluntary poverty—tantamount to Sin in the U.S. of the post/atomic period—outside, that is, the SYNTHETIC/MECHANO/ORGANIZATION of biochemic life, in desperate WILL TO BELIEVE in themselves as much more than ciphers in the proverbial metallic filing cabinets of the jerry/built/junk/sustained MATERIALIST VOID. We took to the streets and inner temples of Being, we listened to Bird Charles Parker's music, for the musical level was a great Origin point during the late forties and early fifties, WHERE *IT* WAS HAPPENING, as it began to happen in the world of images with the painting of Sheri Martinelli, Iris Brody, and Ronald Bladen, in the sculpture of Bruce Conner, and in the inventive genius of Harry Smith's "time slow/down" 3/dimensional movies.

Now, the poets of this generation have made a singular advance in the AmerEnglish Language and write at a new peak of revolution and renaissance of the language noted to have begun around 1910. Gogo Nesbit, John Hoffman, John Wieners, Gregory Corso, Carl Solomon, Michael McClure, Gary Snyder, Allen Ginsberg, and Blackburn, Olson, and Kerouac have, each in their individual NEW TURNINGS of the language, made poetry GO ON since 1946. Paolo Lionni, 22, in New York continues this movement as many of the abovementioned poets CONTINUE TO TURN ON THE NEW LANGUAGE.

We go to the end of the apocalypse. It IS COME—: AnaAlbion. AmerEnglish poetry awaits the time of Bards, Seers, Oracles, Singers, *the old made new*, the return of Quetzelcoatl, the realization of Artaud's spectacle, the Divine Intervention, General Mutation, Destruction/Re/Creation of civilization, the Return of Gitchi Manito uniting the Americas from Alaska to Tierra del Fuego, anti/politics of Sudden Enlightenment, biochemic/sidereal mutation, earthquakes, deluges, transfiguration of the earth—THE TIME OF THE SAINTS! THE REIGN OF THE HOLY! Anything else is just an evil/corny/stupid/sick hell, and we are not staying in hell but have come out of it, for the first time in a hundred years—mark THAT!, angel eyes!

++++++++ fin ++++++++

MENTAL CEMENT

Time: Virgo, 1963. Place: Bay of Tangier: in our shirts wafted by warm atlantean breath, Guy Harloff spoke, within an hour of first meeting (I was leaving for *Kemet*) of an enormous number of cosmogonies, legends, texts, epiphanies, voyages; he traversed three "weirs" of mutual interest: Lovecraft's stories, Meyrink's novels and the writings of the alchemist known as "The Cosmopolitan." Lovecraft "struck home": the American descendent of Poe who, by ignoring rationalistic machine/science of early 20th century, rediscovered truth and marvels *under the earth*. Several months later, I was re-reading "The Call of Cthulu," a tour-de-force of surreal archaeology.

INTERSECTION POINT: Harloff's eye/combustions *fix* certain definite correspondences between popular North-African design & cigar-bands ... masonic triangles & baseball diamonds: paintings, collages, illuminations of *this* & *that* time, squared and circled by traditional "symboliques" and cemented, by mind, via bold word/explosions bordering and exclamating his break/thru from beyond the world of painting. By primal motifs, Harloff reveals the brain of poetry, sometimes obviously and other times, distortedly, essentially reflecting the precise canons of the variegated, but nonetheless universal, Gnosis. This plastic re-assertion of antique signs & numbers happens to be an accurate cartography to the prevailing shift/in/consciousness increasingly evident since the world ended around 1961, ushering in a "time" not unlike, by cyclic seismograph, the 18th century which replete with "aerial prodigies" equals "flying saucers," le Comte de Saint-Germain connects to 1927—V.I.P. year, rumors of Magic translate to neo-Planckian time/space, as geophysical years contact "living mythos" and archaeology rediscovers "the rites of number."

The message continues and is always arriving, traceable from Bosch to Max Ernst, gathering further Harloffian force, on its way to pointing out future traditions. We are, again, at the cross-roads wherein Ancient Tradition intersects contemporary techniques and Harloff's visual statement makes a *signature* for that realm that defies absolute analysis, overturns mere psychology and essentially rests on a theocentric & geocentric understanding of the processes within Nature, the invisible scales weighing, as always, the important essences breaking into the sphere of Happenings: Here is the moving mirror stretched across jet-lined orbits from X to Y and other points *Going East*.

Harloff has written by plastic wand on the Air of this time: IL N'EST PAS TROP TARD. Yes, never too late to Affirm and ReDiscover, as he has recently, the vital necessity of WORK, SECRET POWER and the marvelous exfoliations of the Unflinching Eye of precise MEASURE.

Morocco, Gemini, 1964

REVELATNEWSPORT
BY RAPHAEL KOHLER

2 USA BLACKS & 1 SEEREPORTER BUSTED BY MOROCCANS FOR HOLDING KIF!!

Court Judges: "Kif's prohibited ..... isn't it also in your country?"

R. Kohler's offense: possession ¼ oz kif
Grievance: lost time & $60 fine

TANGIER/scape
May 28 June 2 1964
(dedacatable US State Dept)

Here I am out of Casbah "black hold of Calcutta" movie/Prison 5 day bit 200 Berbers & us sweating sardines urinalysis slop/soup moonshaped liquidy breads Sprawled & sleeping bodies heads to toes feet to hips thigh-Clashings crammed on all sides daily several flare ups tank/violence early-morning "tensions" SAVAGE

Social comment point 53 over age IQ's/8 out of 200 bow to Mecca traditional times a day majority put Prayer DOWN and dig LUSHING fistfighting & maniacal wrestling COLLECTIVE HORSING/AROUND Most of these monkeys unconscious fags making their days & nights by much muscular pretensions cribbed from '30s & '40s Hollywood pop/cult & toughguy put ons fed them from American "aid to the underdeveloped" Now Moroccans proof/positive SOLD ON LAPPING UP USA MACHINE/VIEWS & TV MAGICKS, etc.

e.g. purple jeans & beige over coats while traditional jellaba wearing rapidly disappears Whole antikif Bag has full ruling consent of 10% Moroccans i.e. lite rate ArabLeague flunkys who CAN & SHALL & DO SELL MAJORITY PLASTIC GIMICKS AS ONCE THEY SOLD THEM ALLAH!

**

"Hell Hole" first & lasting impression we have of the joint Some murderers mixed in with us most Moroccans here for petty thefts.

Since Independence few yrs back from France & Spain the country progressively undergoing deprivation & dire poverty Many Tangerines having lost wealth from end of internationalCity Status prefer 2 sloppail meals & jail pallets to no/food nor any place to pad Hence superover crowds of this & rumored other prisons e.g. overfull Holds at Laroche, Rabat, Cassablanca

Lots of suspected & actual Terrorists operating—saw innumerable policevans a day pick up ZoccoChico people, expecially active FuzzRoundUps just before King makes his annual visits.

ITEM: 1 shithouse for all of us containing 2 latrines! no toilet paper/of course/ just wipe off yr ass with tapwater from the corner Havent eaten enuf anyway but how long can you fast and my 2 compatriots are sentenced 3 months Better be fully Ascetic before you try this bag!

* * *

This fuckdup social cultural TURNOVER since Moroccan Independence APES comically but mostly PERVERSELY Official USA REPRESSION & SUPPRESSION LINES mis/educating once relatively untainted/naturalistic peoples to ANTI/Sex NON/freedoms increasing strong PUTDOWN OF CUSTOMARY KIF SMOKING while PUTTINGUP Government/TAXABLE ALCOHOL CONSUMPTION!

* * * *

Newest manifestations parallel cleanup of "beatniks" Rabat-directed with at least tacit approval of US State Dept about 40 mostly americans deported & jailed 2 months ago
EQUATE to
alcohol tolerance among Muslims plainly forbidden by Koran which is actually inprocess of social NON/APPLICATION inside most Arabruled nations .... 3 beers enuf to get Moroccans raving & fighting even up to quasi/murder/moods! All this topt with unprecedented harassment of for-

eign homosexuals once tolerated in preIndependent days Now Moroccans suddenly begin adopting American European moralistic Attitudes about sexual preference activities ITEM: English photographer sentenced 5 years local Prison for posing & printing pictures of natives in various balling positions .... Actually there's whole tribe in South M. goes in for periodic Erotic Orgies ..... so new scenes Goes In AmerEurop Style while old North African Customs fall by wayside apropos Eroticism here's a folksy saying out of the Sahara heard few yrs back: "A woman is fine a boy sheer delight BUT A MELON IS DIVINE!"

*****

Passing time in joint two middle class/type spades & I chat ecstatically about Black Muslims pro & con ..... and ..... is Cecil Taylor our greatest jazzman or not? & how Jazz Music can someday get to CONSTANT SWING LEVELS not unlike—in their way—Indian Raga Music is on ReCord doing NOW! i.e. after 5,000 yr traditional evolution Feeling & Teckne having achieved point of universal musical superiority Paul Bowles & I recently agreed "Raga Music definitely Greatest music in existence" I say: mebe 300 years from now by consciously-controlled non/commercial Evolution & Dremevolutions Jazz MIGHT COULD make it to SUPER/PERFECT CELESTIAL LEVELS OF CONSTANT SWING ....

Cecil Bird & Others before & now actually prophets of JAZZ/FUTURE remember out of mere 100 yr line .... later listening to Miles I know he & most jazz musicians incapable of CONSTANT SWING TOTAL LIFE EXPRESSION which you can only get from RAGAS It's simply lack of POET DIRECTION FROM HIGHEST CONSCIOUS CENTERS Meanwhile S.G. on Tangier streetcorner Meet sez "3 yrs enuf" for this kind of Evolution IF right Conditions Rite Conditions PREVAILED to SPEEDUP REALIZATION OF LONG OVERDUE POETMAN MAGIAN *IRAWAKA* "Irawaka" original phonetics for what Frenchied came out as "Iroquois" civilized NorthAmerican INDIAN NAME FOR OUR NATION instead of erroneus cartographic conventional name "America" Cross Reference for those interested: Italian-Mexican scholar Guttiere Tibon's "America 40 Siglos de la Historia de una Palabra" & for general information Longfellow's HIAWATHA still basic poetic text along with Smithsonian Institute Ethnological reports & transcriptions from first & continuing white/men & Indian encounters... These & other textual sources have relayed explicit necessity TO NAME THE NATION CORRECTLY & TRULY & POETICALLY e.g. "Mexicans," "Canadians," "Peruvians" all names derived from American Indian sources for specific regions already in current usage only WE DONT HAVE A NAME WHO INHABIT THAT REGION BETWEEN CANADA & MEXICO & THE CARIB ISLES BETWIXT PACIFIC & ATLANTIC ...... WATCH FOR further RevelatNewsSupplement & SeerSearch Study *FOUNDATIONS OF IRAWAKA* poet Philip Lamantia rumored compiling from Europe ....

******

SPECIAL CUTUP FROM SOOTHSAYER'S POST/JOINT ILLUMINATION

Project Irawaka

Number 1 SeerPort Manifestation I

IT SHALL HAPPEN: Full TurnOn
Nothing Ever Heard Before It ... SOUNDS!
Necessary come/backs, personages,
rhythms & structures : : :

Fu Manchu as Chief Crazy Horse doubling for Count of SaintGermain
reputedly on scene for FIRST DECLARATION OF INDEPENDENCE & US
CONSTITUTION
& all of IT DREMEVOLUTION BY
LAMONT CRANSTON

       O TE TE TE TE

               ....MOP!

COMING LIQUIDATIONS:

BigBiz Monopols & organised Relig Powers ...... OUT! CONSTANT BIRTH
CONTROL ...... IN! siphon BC Chemic thru general watersupplies sez WB
   results: NO MORE BABIES ONTO ZERO BIRTH RATE 1970!
.... wombs for balling ONLY!

ABOLITION OF POLITICALCuntPower

REGENERATION OF HIGHEST MALE

HEAD & HEART CENTERS RADIATING RULER SHIP BY MAGICAL CREATION DREMEVOLUTION
psychocastrated/boys OUT! ROYAL MEN AT HELM OF CREATIVE STATE running along general TAOIST LINES/cross-reference "Tao Teh Ching" & other texts—pythagorean-buddhist-American Indian philosophy-et al—for skeletonic suggestion blueprints MOST OF ALL SEE INNER & OUTER KNOWLEDGE TELEKINETIC CONTACT WAY FOR IT . . .

Yr seerporter suggests also his individual bit gleamed out of turn/on & serious study of LUXOR PHARONIC GEO-METRIC TEKNE wherein can be found FOUNDATION FOR FUTURE SITE *Synthesis* of poetry/magic/philosophy/science
become HIGHEST ART FORM of NEW GLYPH & GOING TOWARDS SOMETHING LIKE TAOIST FORMULA OF "THE UNCARVED BLOCK"

****

ALL CREATIVE BRAINS UNITE you have nothing to lose but yr frights! From BEGINNING we WRITERS made & now make everything HAPPEN—all that was & is & shall be came about BY OF & FOR CREATIVE/GENIOUS & those not/creating CAN therefor LEARN TO READ THOSE WHO ARE MAKING IT HAPPEN until YES! "poetry made by all"
(Lautréamont wrote over 100 yrs ago . . . . . state of life long, long OVERDUE!)

Those now living go on living Comes to everybody left SWINGS ON CREATIVE/MAGIAN WAY become PoetMen & Poet's Women WORLD! Simple easy intelligent dissolutions formulas & SOLUTIONS ..... right? Yes ... well I'm writing it in for you now friends & enemies—"one inside the other" i.e. LIQUIDATE START LIQUIDATING NOW FOLLOWING HANGUPS.

"arguments" contentions sex/battles blood-mind cancers hacked/souls inhuman deprivations stupidCuntGoofs miseries of biochemical origins clotures/non/clotures
LIQUIDATE NOW bought/governments

middle/class inanit/insanities NO MORE "adjustments" phonywars "revolutions" "frontiers" phonier big/biz cumafiaEconolutions built/in liberal/labor "dissents" OUT FOREVER WITH SICKY PSYCHO & CORPUS—as cool William sayeth "Come ONE SWINGING ORGANISM"

Infacto MINUS SIGN FOR X/Generations multiplied by further MINUS until you have ROYAL CEREBRAL CORTEX TRANSMUTATIONS INSTIGATED BY MAKER'S GOD/ZAP EMPIRES OFF EXISTENCE WHEELS & OUT OUT OUT TIPI HOLE TO
"MAGIAN HIP SITES"
i.e. LaoTza's Chinese word for GREAT is GOING BACK & GOING FARTHER OUT .... equals Albion as Acquarias equals taoist Water formula equals Blake's GIANT MIGRATED TO AMERICA! equals One Language Communication Center by Maker's MEANING/STATE

ITEM/note Greek word for poet is MAKER—more ancient original Western Archive uniting highest ART OF MAKING is the CORRECT READING OF EGYPTIAN GLYPH—the Neter known as THOTH or "ThriceGreat" HERMES translated into latin as MERCURY, strength of LITTLE FINGER OF HUMAN HAND/as I stab exclamations stops periods dots asterisks crosses minuses et al

????///////————++++++++++THUS!.......

///////////////////////

end of message UNO

Watch for future RevelatNewsPorts & Digests in EverySEERSInCommunication PICT/MAG....

September 1775

* * * * * * * * * * *

—Back to

RevelatROUNDUP

* * * * * * *

Tangier June 2 1964

Police cut me loose 5 days later idiotgrins & stinking indigenes food so bad I hallucinated hourly.

personal Ramadan mint tea tasted like liquid glu

TANGIER IS OUT, mohn!

LIKE

the two USA Blacks offense was holding 25 kilos kif for which they were beaten INQUISITION/style water torture suspended upsidedown&blindfolded   /NINE Moroccan Police hitting their Stomaks lungs Heads & stick-Whipping em under soles of the Feet!

      quote them
    "HUNG UP LIKE SHEEP"

Later/cynic/type put it like this: "Moroccan police get their licks like French did to them before Independence..."

A wise word to hippies everywhere:

     YugoSlavLiners GO ON
        &
     ON
       DONT STOP HERE!

...... sincerely yr humble RevelatPorter RETURNED
        by Gitchi Manito
         as 2FacedWEIRD
north/south Axis Going EAST by ZAP/ARK ARK

& to the West with love . . . . .

NEXT INSTALLMENT onto 1799

|*END*|
*

1964/1968

NOTES TOWARDS A POETICS OF WEIR

Dear Bob Hawley:

Certain practical matters—including short trip to Gibraltar—caused some delay in finalizing the [*Touch of the Marvelous*] MS; but here it is!—including special dedication, statement by Parker Tyler, chronology & biograph for dust/jacket&photo. I hope you will find it as interesting to read & publish as your anticipatory enthusiasm inferred. At least, I think it is a great improvement over my first book—by continuity & selectivity which by deletion on one hand unifies the mainstream of that period and by addition of two other sections, aptly qualified by the two section/titles, marks development & tangents—since it contains, also, about 15 pages never before collected (*Erotic Poems* was, incidentally, someone else's suggested title!) as well as carrying a poem "The Image of Ardor"—recovered from Mr. Tyler—never before published! If I hadn't, as the biograph relates, "burnt manuscripts" from that time I certainly might have had much more to represent those years; however, I do feel that qualitatively the best I have to show for first 7 years does actually appear between the pages of the present MS. Having re/acquainted myself with the work during these past few weeks, I've been led to wonder just how much, also, of the "lost" work might actually finally be recovered. I remember many instances sending copies to editors & friends (perhaps never recovered as in Tyler's case, to whom I made such a request on a hunch a few weeks ago!) which I could very well attempt to contact in the future, not surely for the present edition, but perhaps for a future OYEZ edition, if indeed you also continue over the years … who knows, perhaps a further, more compendious, edition of early work can be realized? Altogether, it has been a vital experience editing *Touch of the Marvelous* and you will excuse this possible nostalgia on my part!

* * *

I have—except for deletion of superfluous punctuation—kept the poems almost exactly as the originals. This may look somewhat old/fashioned at times—the hyphens for one thing & often poems with capitalized first letters—but it retains the spirit of youthful unconcern thereby with what are, I still think, very minor technicalities. The more important matter of linear & stanza structure I have adhered to absolutely—except, again, in a few minor places—where it is a question of retaining the "formal" coherence of rhythm & sense. Nevertheless, I suspect the general "linguistic" definition of poetry as "a certain highly *concentrated* language"—in contradistinction to the "more *loosely* concentrated one of prose"—to be generally correct, in so far as one can recognize the poetry as such even if it were presented as "conventional prose."

As was the case with the bulk of this present MS, the poems were a direct & rapid transcription from certain states of *trance* and I personally considered it a fault to alter anything but misspellings or excessive & therefore distracting grammatical errors, convinced as I was then of the orthodox surrealist dictum going something like: "... thought's dictation in the absence of all conscious control & censorship...."

But it is—more so after the passage of two decades of further poetic experience & experiment—that the essential vitality of this manner of writing is due to a general synthesis of feeling & ideas which profoundly directed the aforementioned "method" and this I entertained & pursued as a *conscious aim*, the effects of which established a *rhythm of incongruous imagery*, a prosodic mystique, so no matter to what formal arrangement I subjected the flow of images to afterwards, if I remained faithful to the primary condition of releasing the images from a heightened state of trance, through the sluicegates of "contradiction" and incongruity, the possibility existed and still exists of making a significant kind of Revelation. Though the orthodox surrealist definition & practice associated this with a revelation of the Unconscious and generally conceded to characterize states of dream, hallucination, fantastic/juxtaposition, etc., I find more interest in recognizing a far/wider meaning & value than the now/academic categories—Freudian or Jungian—to the degree that such poetry & its attendant prosody does *reveal* through *the music of incongruity* & imagery of the non-rational, vital "rapports" of a direct, intuitional comprehension of Reality—beyond "logical-rationalist" or common-sense appearances—otherwise unrepresented except in the vaguest "mystical" or didactic descriptions which often fail miserably because they are founded on a process of making common/sense logical statement of human experience & understanding which is ultimately non-rational, connected, as it is, to a *source and cause* which is beyond linguistic definition or presentation! See, in this respect, a very pertinent line in the poem "A Winter Day" which also could serve as emblem for this book: "... a whole world which seems to go beyond its own existence." Precisely! It is, then, a poetry most definitely of the world of appearances but giving—by the very juxtaposition of images/in/apparent/contradiction—form to a universal aspiration: quest & need for evolution to a higher state of consciousness, naturally *evoked* by a certain rhythm & language of incongruity, fantastic juxtaposition of images & thoughts, often the speech of trance, but also opening up possibility of a consciously/directed Evocation of the Something & SomeWhereElse sensed generally as source/cause of all existence, being & becoming! This I believe again remains a fecund enough direction, *now*—unencumbered by merely relativist "surrealist" or "Jungian" ideas; an ever/verdant Vehicle of Amazing Marvels which I have christened elsewhere as "WEIR," both as recall to one of the supreme ancestors of this pursuit—Poe—& in order to evoke further progressions in this time & beyond. I am convinced, no matter what new "names" for it manifest, that what I am talking about (and for which *Touch of the Marvelous* can serve as, at least, one seminal model) is a vital vein in western thought & art, rooted in a most ancient Tradition rarely understood even today, yet recognized, generally, by a few, as "the Mediterranean genius of Analogy": our fundamental poetic heritage & most distinctive western line of apprehending reality which, at this reading, I have come to understand bears by vital cognition the key to "vital laws of Harmony" throughout the universe: For it is in the rapport of "things different from one another" that the poet reveals & communicates his *vision* commingling the visible & invisible, the heard & unheard, seen & unseen, intuitive and cerebral knowledge, the concrete & abstract; hence: the purely sensorial level of apprehension connected to the *inborn, instinctive, cordial* & *supra/harmonic* levels of understanding (prophecy) which *are weir*, a designation/emblem of analogy, a homonym/translation derived from the Latin word "to see" (vidi)!

For me, then, the poet must be the herald of all "*that goes beyond its own existence*," the vital link to the universal order, attested by philosophers & mystics—hence defined only abstractly or not at all—by a deliberate evocation at once representing the world of appearances—or sense/datum—but entirely *transformed*, reversed, vitally "destroyed," turned/up/side/down, if you will, which makes—it is evidentially true!—for an intense poétic experience conveying often the *living* marrow of the BEYOND! Moreover: That Beyond which I insist is the *causal realm* of which the sensible world is the *effect* (not directly the effect, but BY ANALOGY!) ... Therefore a complete re/definition of Analogy must begin. It is not a question of one image to another, aesthetically or cerebrally brought into relation, but of evoking through a consciously understood play of images to reveal the hidden rapports; they may or may not develop according to surrealist rules or any other kinds for that matter, since it is primarily a matter of Hearing & Seeing *in another way* beyond the ordinary, including the "ordinary" fantastical or the too/obvious ornamentally "surreal," that I mean to imply: THE EYES & EARS OF THE HEART IN VITAL TOUCH WITH THE SECRET CENTERS OF THE TEN THOUSAND THINGS! As an example, from the most traditional western source of this very Synthesis, I refer you to the

Sphinx of Egypt itself, one of the most perfect & generally misunderstood surrealist images! There is a pure representation of the SomeWhereElse & the Weir for which Poe's "Ulalume" is, in another instance, the *sonic bridge*!*

* * * * *

1965/1966

---

*EDITOR'S NOTE: A variant of this final paragraph appended to this particular draft of "Notes Towards a Poetics of Weir" reads as follows: "The revelation of a world beyond its own existence: the certainty that together with contemporary knowledge of facts of nature, ordinary logic & reasonings are negligible, the poet guided by an intuition from the depths of his being (his sure guide of inner knowledge) is a herald of a universal order that is never apparent, but only a signature of a text that remains un-readable except by the most special technique of evocation, necessarily "esoteric," the rules of which must be re-covered by a complete shift of consciousness that truly is "SomeWhereElse" by inspiration & essence: somewhere else, that is, than steeped in merely sensorial/factual datum or datum reducible only to social/psychology or physiology: for actually the poet is the Herald of a Realm Beyond Any Sensual or Mechanical Scrutiny: the utterly Beyond, the vital SomeWhereElse which I insist is the causal realm from which the sensible universe is but the effect! A complete re-definition of analogy, other than the academic ones, must be revealed! It is not a matter of an "image" of window being opposed to "another one of brain" and mounting up arbitrarily or aesthetically the "rapport" or lack of rapport (the classic surrealist approach), but of allowing Naturally the Play of Images to Reveal Hidden Rapports which follow the actual interchanges of what the Chinese named "the yin" and "the yang"; it is obvious that a new synthesis of analogy is in formation, which can just extend beyond either the surrealist & non-surrealist procedures; indeed, the Sphinx of Egypt remains for our whole conscious history a monument to this very Synthesis! Poe's "Ulalume" is an ever present sonic/bridge to the SomeWhereElse! There shall appear before this century is completed works of the marvelous for which the over/turn of an Age—I mean: the end of the Piscian period—is evidentially the telling sign! General confusion shall give way again to the Luciferian Light which must never be confused with the over/cerebration of Satan that gives "reasonings", for being & existence via deadly & erroneous superficialities: I affirm absolutely: I HAVE MY BEGINNING & END SOMEWHERELSE: I ATTEMPT THE REVELATION OF THE REALMS OF WEIR!"

TESTAMENT OF THE INTER-VOICE

Poetry is life, i.e., the greater life of man. By *poetry* I mean the transmutation of human desire into a higher form of existence than its so-called "natural" state, manifested visibly in the poetic imagination and in the transformative poetic act. The imagination, it must be understood, is an autonomous & mysterious elemental *power* within all of us, the "maker of images" elementally, but whose extensive liberation is a power of the nth degree, determining *a possible transmutation of psycho-biologic life*! Under the auspices of a certain interior voice, the voice—as André Breton so beautifully said—"that ceases not above the raging of the storms and goes on even to beyond death," this power of image-manifestation can be rendered as a superior instrument of self-creation and a way of life superior to the derivative & watered-down "mystiques" & "yogas," et al., sources all the more suspect as they negate the unity of natural and unknown powers within us in preference for some "quiescent void," the opposite of vitality and of liberating power. The universe is ultimately unknown, its source and aim incomprehensible to reason and no "void" can shed light on its nature; the "void" understood and discernible in natural phenomena can be represented by the knot on a tree which has gnarled & ceased to bear fruit or branch; we cannot expect enlightenment from this "stage" analogous to our psychic voids and the famous "emptiness" of mystics is no more than a stage, preliminary, perhaps, to "new life" coming forth at some other level of the trunk of the tree! There is a kind of absolute knowledge which refuses cerebral & rational forms of comprehension but which *living poetry*—poetry *lived*—may reveal; by imaginative transmutation, a poem or image—painted, sculpted, or written—gives testament and is a sign of direct knowledge-in-being. Glimpsed even so at times, beneath the layers of our so-called rational & cerebral consciousness, is a beam of unflinching light from which images issue and it's from here the poet is born to manifest by *meditation* their inter-play; it is essential that the poet allow the inter-play of images from these depths of being, hence fulfilling the inborn power of imagination to combine these dimly seen images; for there is a voice there too, in this *place*, within us all, which seems to speak their absolute manifestation always "original" and analogic, uniting the most opposite of images in new synthesis & unity—the *materia prima* of language, it is—and all wisdom is to listen and *mediate* the transmission purely of this original and originating and inexhaustible realm of being from which all we have and know has come!

(1/8/68)

INTRODUCTION TO
THE WOUNDED MATTRESS (1970)
BY SOTÈRE TORREGIAN

I can hear for the first time since autumn the wild cry of the peacocks from the zoo a few blocks from this house which has been graced with your collages and calligraphy and now ... *The Wounded Mattress*. The peacocks of spring. Nancy and I hunted for wayward feathers on many visits to this zoo, but still no success. Nevertheless, brother surrealist, the Overcast the Mists & Snows of winter-past and certain terrible tensions (within me) had made my fingers unable to tell you how much I have appreciated your communications—except vocally via Bell and perhaps, telepathically.

The Wounded Mattress I have been reading and re-reading. So far I have written this:

> Sotère's poetry: The strangeness of cities, spontaneous dream-imagery interjections, vital flames of violet mouths and the presence of woman-trees waking with immortal harmony in chaotic cities. A sempiternal voice of the real-more-than-sensorial-real, the sur-real extension of unimpeded song between the

contradiction of images, true vessel of magical coincidence, Torregian's poems testify for the latest generation to the splendor of the unfettered imagination as the central sun of poetry.

Seattle
March 21, 1969

PHILIP LAMANTIA

I am of Sicilian parentage, born 1927 in San Francisco, California near the XVIIth century Spanish foundations of Mission Dolores. My first poetic hallucination-ecstasy occurred when I identified, in a cradle, the word *"light"* with the electric bulb above my head. I have a clearly engraved image of this initiatory event from which my poetic life seems to proceed. Then came an early fever vision (before seven) in the apparition of a radiating blue-gowned woman from the door of a bedroom closet. When I was fifteen a page of my poems appeared in *View* across from E. E. Cummings on another page. Attracted by the strange beauty of Poe's poetry I had for almost a year written a vast amount of poems but it was not until my chance encounter with surrealism that I seriously considered myself a poet. Not long after discovering *View* I learned of the authentic organ of surrealism in America: *VVV* whose editorial advisors were André Breton, Max Ernst, and Marcel Duchamp. I sent poems and Breton agreed to publish them but requested a letter from me clarifying my position to surrealism. When published in the last issue of *VVV* this letter bore the title "Surrealism in 1943." It is a peculiarly prophetic testament to my later, divergent development and—I am happy to say now—of my ultimate "return" to surreality since

1966 when I again began the arduous and exciting attempt at purely automatic writing as defined by Breton in his *Manifestos of Surrealism* of 1924 and 1929.

By 1946 having broken with surrealism and under baleful influences I began a long interior odyssey that now seems no more than a reaction against the impact surrealism had for me originally. My life and poems (most of which were destroyed by me later) had only occasional or, at best, residual connections to surreality. In the late forties I went to lectures in medieval & oriental studies at the University of California; plunged into the jazz scene in cross-country nomadism; went to Morocco for psychedelic experiences; with other "white Indians" participated in a Washo Peyote Rite. Married for a while to the poetess Gogo Nesbit I left with her for Mexico and later visited the *Coras*, a remote tribe in the Nayarit mountains (see Lumholtz's *Unknown Mexico*); in 1955 rejoined the Catholic Rite of my ancestors and didn't terminate this strangest contradiction to poetry until six years later following on nine months of gratuitous fasting and clairvoyant experiences. Associated with "the beats" I had been one of the poets in the mid-fifties to read with Ginsberg at the famous "6 Gallery Reading."

In 1963 living in Andalusia within the matrix of a small group of friends who had come together for this purpose, I was introduced to specialized studies of myth, philosophy, and mathematics which continued to be my primary activity for the five years I lived in Spain, Morocco, Italy, Greece, and France. I returned to America in 1968 to live in Seattle until the summer of 1969. Now again on San Francisco's Telegraph Hill.

I believe surrealist automaticism to be the basic discovery and activity that bridges the gap between the unconscious and conscious levels of being, between the poetic marvelous and the arbitrary, the dream and concrete reality, the fantastic and the seemingly ordinary. Therefore automaticism is the only path of discovery for the poetic revelation of man in his totality. Indeed I have come to the realization that pure surrealist poetry in our century is the only fundamentally *new* and original development since the beginnings of recorded literature.

1970

STATEMENT FOR CONTEMPORARY POETS OF THE ENGLISH LANGUAGE (1970)

I consider myself essentially a surrealist, but as Breton qualified this, it is *not* a "school," but a way of life.

I understand the act of poetry as the maximum volatile expression of Imagination, a *central power*, relating all levels of conscious and unconscious thought and being. I believe in poetry as a means of unqualified individual liberation. I believe in the poetry of primal melody and the revelation of the mysteries of cosmic being.

1970

BETWEEN THE GULFS

I have watched the metamorphosis of a theory of "volatile-negative-analogies" rise through a group of poems bearing the title *Becoming Visible*, in the sense of releasing out of darkness the words *desiring* movement with other words in a free interchange and development of their properties and signatures, but within a process stalked by the emotion-radiant, palpitant activity that magnetizes the illimitable resources of the arbitrary—a risk-laden region from which the exigent action of unprecedented verbal encounters relates to the refusal of previously known paths of association. Here at the center of a void inundated by a shadow of flashing color, the necessity of the voice released by psychic automatism to find its body provokes the primal spark of dynamic movement while the great "negativistic hand" André Breton exalted as an essential lever of poetic vitality opens dialectically the window on the Heraclitian plane of "the hidden harmonies." Armed with this negative power, writing becomes a rigorous reconstruction against the past, an adamant refusal to be entangled in previously conquered areas of association. From this vista of dormant volcanos and tropical ice, we can all the more happily trace our inspirations from Lautréamont and Rimbaud to Breton and Péret and Roussel to Magloire-Saint-Aude, exemplary signposts for further transgressions, without literally re-tracing in one's own poetic praxis their inimitable movements. The vitality of automatistic progression from this negative summit renders ineffectual the efforts of academic and literary—commodity fetish—assimilation of surrealism's *becoming*, exposing the absurd nature of conventional aesthetic criteria, that farce of the dead hand of "positive identity." The CIA of the mind shall be desiccated in its attempts to stigmatize the latent furor in the great deserts to be overturned.

By Elective Affinities, Then and Now

From having initially found the key (the road opening, 1943–1946) to having lost the key (the road closed down, 1946–1966) and since rediscovering the key (the road re-opening in 1967): my solidarity with the surrealist movement, represented in this time and place by *Arsenal*, reinvents itself without the slightest ambiguity.

1973

VITAL CONFLAGRATIONS

It's true that I don't know how to really live; I have never completely gotten the hang of life, even though the "red phase" of the "Great Work"—radiating a splendor signifying, for some of us, all that *perfects* the gifts of the Marvelous for humanity—haunts the blackening thought of the absence of a certain social oxygen within present-day life. For it is only in sight of the most extravagant utopias (well-seasoned by the repeated claw-marks of potential power splashing on a pinch of high voltage momentarily negating the daily horrors of *attempted* life) and only by absolute confidence in the *surpassing fire* love shall not fail to collectively materialize in the carbonization of the libertines of liberty, that I dream of the living emancipation, kindled from a *preserving fire* of which the surpassing conflagration is the permanent, generating agent.

1973

THE CRIME OF POETRY

Fabre d'Olivet, prodigious philologist of the early 19th century, contradicted the classical-academic etymology of the words "poetry" and "poet" as, respectively, "making" and "maker," thereby superseding the false consciousness exuding from connotations of this dictionary and literary "definition" persisting to this day even among the allegedly "avant-garde." Fabre d'Olivet's erudition discovered that the Greek word for poetry derived from the Phoenician which translated signifies: *"the superior principle of language."* Developing correspondences with this central etymological key in the lengthy preface ("The Essence and Form of Poetry") to his book, *The Golden Verses of Pythagoras*, Fabre d'Olivet signaled his profound agreement with the poetics of Sir Francis Bacon who, from the following viewpoint, can be justly claimed as a precursor of surrealism: "Poetry does truly refer to the Imagination, which may at pleasure join that which nature has severed and sever that which nature has joined and so make unlawful matches and divorces of things ... it does raise and erect the mind by submitting the show of things to the desires of the mind, whereas reason does buckle and bow the mind to the nature of things." Rejecting "craftsmanship," the surrealist viewpoint, respecting sovereignty of mind, the primacy of human desires and oneiric exaltation, considers and finds true poetry to be an instrument of knowledge, of discovery, of unveiling, and of human freedom. Authentic poetry is certainly the highest principle of language, but one which has generally been lost and which surrealism aims to restore, illuminating André Breton's saying: "Language has been given to man so that he may make surrealist use of it," together with Benjamin Péret's genial affirmation, "poetry is the source and crown of all thought." Surrealism's fifty years of poetic evidence demonstrate the initial steps taken towards this supreme *disalienation* of humanity with its language, an emancipatory leap in opposition to the civilized debasement and fragmentation of language by reason, that is, language conditioned to serve as aesthetic object, submission-to-reality, national chauvinism, entertainment, neo-formal energy-fields, stylization, mirror-trickery, everyday speech, pseudo-revolutionary mystification, personal confession, conscious self-expression, and other idiocies—all of which, I insist, can be summed up in the self-condemned monstrosity that was Ezra Pound, his worthless emulators, and what generally passes for poetry and good writing in this country.

Furthermore, the object of surrealism is *moral*. The demands it may elicit from you do not fall short of a furious revolutionary perspective concerning language, poetry, love, science, erotism, politics, dependent on an imaginative exaltation of disquieting materials and potential renewal of latent powers requiring a purification of means well within your grasp, *as easy as the day swallowing the night.*

1974

HARMONIAN RESEARCH

If you are deliriously (and seriously) attracted to the principled expressions of surrealism revealed in the pages of *The Surrealist Movement in the United States* and desire to take preliminary steps toward liaison (assuming knowledge of, and your vital affinity to, the basic principles of the movement and *attending occultation*, found, to mention only the most available texts, in Breton's *Manifestoes* and *Surrealism and Painting*) you are invited, *at the risk of your present life*, to correspond with us by furnishing a comprehensive statement of your understanding of surrealism, indicating the forms of your co-relatable motivation, experiences, and potential contribution. Replies may be expected only if terms of the invitation are coherently fulfilled through which the desired reciprocity can germinate a significant complicity.

1974

THE ONEIRIC LIGHT OF ALICE FARLEY

As I watched Alice Farley's *Fortunate Light*,* I thought of *oneiric light*. This presence of what may be called the webbing of dream activity, its omniscient glow, was surprisingly assisted by the concrete psychologism which inspired the lyrical-erotic gestures of her choreography. One possibility of an authentic *surrealist* dance depends upon projecting this "dream-web," itself the branching of a profound psychic automatism, thereby fulfilling the conditions of arousing a veritable trance-state. As well, I became aware of conceptions transporting a sustained atmosphere once conjured plastically by the early de Chirico and as if his enigmatic "personages" magically encountered the metamorphic geologies of Tanguy's auroral spaces. Transcending the formalities of dance, Alice Farley's ideational content—implying the dictatorship of the marvelous and the central power of imaginary deformations—presents, on a plane rarely explored, a state of disquieting relations in space, germinations of a poeticized space of dynamic analogies, and *becomes poetry itself moving visibly*.

*LAMANTIA'S NOTE: Title of her choreographic transformation performed at the Band Shell in Golden Gate Park in San Francisco, June 1, 1974.

1975

POETIC MATTERS

A concerted abandonment of fixed forms (from sonnets to free verse), rhyme and metrical references cannot be considered anything but a formal change unless it is intrinsically correlative to a high degree of *deformation*, the term suggested by Gaston Bachelard in order to do away with the mistaken notion of "image making" or "image building" which conventional thought has ascribed to the word *imagination*. I cannot help agreeing with Bachelard that the imaginative faculty must be understood as *freeing us from the immediate images of perception* and in his words "without an unexpected union of images, there is no imagination, no imaginative action." He suggests the word "corresponding to imagination is not *image*, but *imaginary* ... that the value of an image is measured by the extent of its imaginary radiance." Now, it is incontrovertible (in accordance with Hegel's findings in *The Philosophy of Fine Art*) that the "*unfettered imagination*" is the basis for poetry, "imaginary content," its objectivity. Rigorously, imaginary power is central to poetic materialization which surrealism locates as a conduit for thought, speech being no more than a mediational instrument that imaginary thought transforms by the deforming of imagery.

But most American poets have mistakenly subordinated the imaginative faculty to the predominance of perception conjoining a slavish reduction of language to "speech patterns" and pragmatic usages. Bachelard characterizes an image which takes on a "definitive form" as assuming "present perception"... such a "stable and completed image *clips the wings of the imagination.* It makes us fall from that dreaming imagination which does not confine itself within any image..."

The literary practitioners of the "post-Olson generation" (as some promoters now label it) have been to a hopeless degree failures on the imaginative and lyrical planes of true poetry, preoccupied as they are with a self-conscious acquiescence to the debasement of language characterizing its reification by technicians and mind-managers of latter-day capitalism.* This direction is glorified specifically in those false poets who pride themselves on a formalized "handling" of "ordinary American speech" which is, in effect, nothing other than a rhetorical camouflage for the betrayal of poetic exigencies in the service of cultural chauvinism and the oppressive "reality principle," reflecting a pitiful need to be recognized by socially conditioned imbecility. Instead of poetry conceived as a disinterested means of emancipation—tending toward the realization of the objects of desire—we have Charles Olson, with misappropriated scientific jargon, reducing "the poem" to unqualified abstractions, "energy" and "energy-discharge," and pontificating the following inane dogma: "one perception must immediately and directly lead to a further perception." Bachelard—scientist in poetry and psychologist of science, champion of Lautréamont and *active imagination*—has noted the crucial distinction between present perception and imagination. The following prescriptive revaluation may be critically situated in

*LAMANTIA'S NOTE: Beyond the general deficiencies of the last thirty years, and outside of the surrealist movement, there are a number of exceptions known to me. Both morally and poetically, for example, there is Bob Kaufman, preeminently; Gregory Corso, who can also be commended for his public disdain of "the Black Mountain School"; and Daniel Moore of *Dawn Visions*. All of these poets share the distinction of having, at certain times, expressed themselves honestly and intensely in a language with real affinities to surrealism.

opposition to all aesthetic ideologies which shift the focus away from poetry's capacity and necessity for imaginative radiance: "To acquire a feeling for the imaginative role of language, we must seek, in every word, the desires for otherness, for double meaning, for metaphor ... we must record all the desires to abandon what we see and what we say for what we imagine. We shall then have some chance of restoring to the imagination its role of attraction. To perceive and imagine are as antithetic as presence and absence. To imagine is to absent oneself; it is a leap toward a new life."

The vociferously alleged "newness" of post-World War II American poetry and poetics associated with Olson, Creeley, Ginsberg, Duncan, Levertov (among the most voluble practitioners and theorizers) pertains to nothing more than a belated "palace revolution" diverging only from the previous literary stranglehold by the fixed-form addicts, a priesthood of feudal minded English professors such as J.C. Ransom, Yvor Winters, and R.P. Warren. The new literary priesthood found one of its main sources in Ezra Pound's glib slogan "Make it New," a recipe which has been actually translated into the advertising, architecture, and designs of "the administered life" as we know it under monopoly capitalism and for which the inventor of futurism, Filippo Marinetti, by 1909, had sounded the exact intellectual tocsin.*

Like Marinetti, Olson posits unqualified "energy" and "the *kinetics* of the thing" as major technical preoccupations for composition. In fact, Marinetti's literary program seems to have resurfaced in Olson's reading of Pound, who asserted that the whole modern movement which he, T.S. Eliot, and Joyce represented as a nucleus had its origins directly in Marinetti's futurism.

*During a sojourn in Rome (1964) I encountered a curious circle of old and young "friends of Marinetti" and became familiar with the substance of the Pound/Marinetti correspondence housed in a special archive. Thus I was able to acquire little-known facts concerning the futurist movement which, by way of explaining its "eclipse," certain of the "amici" hypothesized had as "enemy" none other than surrealism. Pound's fanatical pro-Italian posture corresponded, in fact, to Marinetti's proto-fascist and racist theory of Italian superiority over all other national groups based on the cultural "Genius," which, according to early futurist propaganda, was alleged to be a monopoly of the Italians (!). Finally, Pound's political position, as one of Mussolini's most prestigious supporters, culminated in his Word War II radio broadcasts emphasizing permanent preferences for all things Italian over what Pound considered his own countrymen's inferiority and barbarism. During the Allied invasion of Italy, Pound could be heard over the radio soliciting American soldiers to surrender, invoking Italian cultural and political superiority as the main argument.

There is the curious fact of an aesthetic movement (Italian futurism) proclaiming extreme "novelty" and "dynamism" and all the while seminating, primarily through its founder, political "solutions" that found their end in fascism. At its origins futurism extolled war and extreme patriotism often expressed in organized mass demonstrations as well as in artistic productions; its political program, anti-parliamentarian and anti-socialist, consisted of a germinal theory of organizing the State and the economy which was largely realized later in Mussolini's Corporate State. The proposal that futurist artists and poets should rule society was, of course, less than fruitful. (Even Mussolini's belated appointment of Marinetti as cultural minister in the 1930s had no immediate significant effect on Italy.) However, the translation of certain futurist political proposals into central features of fascism does suggest the preponderant influence of the Marxian model of a "super-structural" ideology interacting on the infra-structure of Italian capitalism at crucially interstitial "moments" before and after World War I and extending considerably thereafter to finally determine a general aesthetic, by reduction and technical adaptations, in the architecture and stylizations which today throughout the world still resemble the futurist models. For it is *not* Picasso's influence, as alleged recently by some pundits of mass opinion, that is evident "all around us" in the contemporary civilized world. (If it were so, then where is the intense lyricism and super-reality represented by Picasso in his most important imaginative works between the two World Wars?) But the fact remains, we have reached the point in 1975 that the act of reading Ginsberg and Olson or any of their epigones is interchangeable with the scanning of *Time* and *Newsweek*. I maintain this is no "accident" but clearly delineates the *false consciousness of poetry* proliferating within the shifting gears of decadent capitalism.

Contrary to the consensus of American literary "authorities" who decided to separate Pound "the man" from "the poet," deploring his fascist politics and hailing his literary achievements, I believe Pound's poetics are as anti-human as his politics and, if his poetry is examined closely, considering the historical facts vis-à-vis Marinetti's futurism, it will be obvious to what extent the two currents interpenetrate. Fascism's claim to "revolution" by the cult of "youth" and "newness" while resuscitating the classicist values of Greco-Roman civilization and concretized, laughingly so, in the architecture known as "Mussolini modern," is a neat similitude to Pound's exclusive and scholastic insistence on Aristotelian logic and his aping of "the classics" while cinematically employing the linguistic idioms of a political ward heeler in the United States of the 1920s.

Charles Fourier rightly judged civilization to be the carrier of oppressive ideologies. In open hostility to the cancerous and moribund moral "values" exemplified in the bourgeois-academic "classics," surrealism prefers the great poetry of the primal peoples of the earth, and recognizes as well signs of revolt and liberty in the heretical, gnostic, and heterodox developments in thought throughout the last three thousand years which significantly diverged from the judeo-christian and academic Greco-Roman traditions. I have always dreamed of the ultimate triumph of the legendary Sirens who, it was said, were "defeated" in their poetic combat with the Muses and who can be deciphered to typify imaginative freedom from the restraints of rationally controlled poetry whose spokesmen, like all good bourgeoisie, must always recommend that we "plug our ears" against the enchantresses heard by the inspired poet on his voyage to the unknown. The great nineteenth century painter, Gustave Moreau, must have known of the heterodox meaning of this legend, since he depicts the poet at the feet of the Siren, evoking her role as a subaqueous source of poetic inspiration, associating humanity's origin with water, which Sándor Ferenczi later found so psychoanalytically significant.

It is not, as with Baudelaire, "plunging into the unknown" to find "the new," by which he who named imagination "the queen of the faculties" implied a path of *descent into oneself*, but, for the American versifiers, a consciously manipulated method of fragmenting reality by reduction to random sensorial (primarily *retinal*) reporting and syntactic distortions suggesting a "newness" sought as an end in itself, much as reactionary versifiers of the late nineteenth century espoused "art for art's sake." Evading completely the primary problems of what it is that *informs content* in poetic practice, the emphasis on technical means which are often enough turned into ends, becomes a delusionary surface structure hiding the fact that poetry, in the sense understood by Hegel as "an act of unfettered imagination," is nowhere to be found. Instead we are given a whole new set of conventions replacing the old ones of rhyme and meter, but whether "projective verse," "cutups," "organic form," "concrete poetry," or "songs à la rock 'n roll," these are merely another group of unmistakably petty "games" Rimbaud so rightly denounced in earlier counterparts and which surrealism has superseded. Just as boring as medieval litanists and "alliteratives," or the sonneteers of a few generations ago, the present "poem makers" come puffing and choking and creaking like the anthropomorphic caricatures of broken-down automobiles depicted in animated cartoons. The rottenness of these dichotomizing and alienating literary dogmas of the last twenty-five years should not fail to become more evident to others as the Surrealist Movement in the United States progresses to initiate a quantitatively determining *lever of revolution* on the cultural plane, since surrealism offers the sole challenge and viable alternative to what amounts to a conspiracy of poetic degeneracy in this country. Such degeneracy (with all its attendant implications) may be illustrated by a dialectical transposition of a recent Ginsberg book title, turning into "The *Fall of Poetry* in America." This "Fall" is the real *kinetic* activity of the post-Olson versifiers, as the mystificatory *poetry equals energy* identity is the reductionist predication of a psychological crisis with its roots in the alienated subject terrified by the repressed images he has successfully evaded during acts of composition.

Instead of words set free from the prosaic prisons of social reality, images transformed by desire, poetry freed from the "laws" of nature, attentive to the becoming of unknown analogies, words purified by the rays of oneiric desire, language emancipated from the confines of speech, informed by the inner ear and disdainful of "music" other than the rhythms immanent in imaginary thinking, analogies whose *encounters* elicit every type of humor—and instead of language becoming a means of infinite imaginary combinations—most established American poets of this century have given us a massive literature of sensibility, self-narration, virtuosity, and literal confessions signed very energetically by the stylus of the death-wish.

∗ ∗ ∗

The only pleasure I can possibly derive from this necessary critique of the bankrupt tendencies in American pseudo-poetry is in proportion to the possibility of an effective *disruption* among the youth who are being oppressed by a programmed set of misdirections and blind alleys projected in the schoolrooms whose categories evoke the names of nauseous adjuncts to bourgeois-bureaucratic culture. The most pernicious and mystifying tendency—and the more pronounced within the last decade—has been the application of the misnomers "surreal" and "surrealistic" to the *sham article*, causing the gravest difficulties among the uninformed and misinformed, a despicable practice which all authentic surrealists everywhere have always denounced. To affirm, for example, as some academician did recently, that "surrealism has become almost anything at all" since it is "the language our poets speak," not only is tendentiously flippant but more seriously represents the blatantly confusionist tactics of a whole gang of literati who have managed to do nothing better than dabble with the surface effects of genuine surrealist expression in order to proffer fake semblances which, for those of us in whom *individual discovery* is a matter of *sustained quest*, can elicit only our entire contempt.

* * *

Surrealism rejects the scaffolding of the priesthoods of Literature and Art pompously sold in the commodity exchanges of schools and museums as "the Classics." Analogous to the bureaucratic mind of political domination is the literary one which comes crowing with its moribund "dominant tendencies," "the spirit of the times," and ejaculations of "talent" and "genius" to characterize this or that travesty of human potential. Rigidity, confusion and mystification, a stultifying provincialism, are the usual hallmarks of this parasitic literary charade played at the expense of any sign of disinterested and unqualified human freedom, for which these *respectable* gangs of the pimps of Literature and Art do their utmost to isolate, if not by a noisy confusionism, then by well-known "conspiracies of silence" and scandal mongering. Each day there appear myriad articles, essays, and other visible means of funneling the promotional lies concerning "reputations," "traditions," and the cabals of "masters" and apprentices of this or that coterie, wrapped in the guise of the inevitable "newness," the predictable fad and fashion perpetrated more than a hundred years since Rimbaud's lucid rejection of "the rotten game of two thousand years!" It is this same rotten game of aesthetic manipulators that pretends to close, except by a sneering recuperation, any insight into those who in the twentieth century carried incandescent and convulsive poetic activity by absolute signs of the Marvelous.

These are our immediate precursors. Samuel Greenberg was one of the most disquieting figures in the twentieth century, one whose great imaginative power is not in the least lessened for his having projected his Promethean reveries within the "romantic" idiom, thereby doubly offering us a glimpse of what is missing in late nineteenth century poetry in America, and gifting us with a view of perturbation and irrepressibility revealing the human condition as Kafka and Alfred Kubin had from other vantage points. Greenberg's tubercular illness is the other side of his salutary intelligence-of-the-heart that sounded, poignantly and radiantly, in poems that are veritable *wounds of wonder* transpiring in those last years of his approaching death in 1917, at age 23, from a bed in the "Sea View Hospital" on Staten Island, and *singing beyond it*.

With Mina Loy's *Lunar Baedeker* (1923) we encounter a singular flowering of what Hegel rightly announced to become *after him* the most fecund vehicle for poetic thought, in its specifically mythic function, and which Jacques Vaché located contemporaneously with Mina Loy's appearance, as *umor*—alternating her subtleties of wit between sensible convulsions in *darkest luminosity*.

In the 1920s Harry Crosby, a true dandy of explosively Promethean desire, left in *The Mad Queen* and elsewhere, signs of a "Sadean" magnanimity in the realms of mad love; before him, in America, perhaps none but Poe, in a few of his most "ectoplasmic" descents (and in the spirit of *Eureka*), comes to mind as purely comparable.

***

As young as tomorrow, throwing its shadow over the moment's irrepressible desires, surrealism is at once what originated through certain historical confluences and astonishing discoveries (enhanced by what has evolved to this moment in systematic exploration and interpretations of the human condition), which came to the *foreground of consciousness* around 1920 in the minds of André Breton and a few of his friends who could assert not long after that they had indeed refound the long-sought "philosophers' stone," in the disinterested revolt of imaginative power capable of demolishing in one stroke any fixed notion of reality. A recent sign of surrealism's historical efficacy was noted where Breton suggested its *permanent birth* "in the genius of youth" who in May 1968 inscribed their watchword on the walls of Paris for all the world's eyes to register: "*All power to the imagination!*"

Since Huizinga's *Homo Ludens* re-established these certain sources for poetry: *play*, *enigma*, and *the hermetic*, we can all the more comprehend surrealism's consistent activation of these three zones of human expression, by liberating the unconditional and disinterested play of imaginary thought, revitalizing the enigmatic, and revealing the concealed. Ultimately, automatism's *raison d'être* is the quest to reveal the latent content of human existence in its entirety.

* * *

In Arizona I was privileged to witness a series of Hopi Indian ceremonies which suggest a *living myth* fulfilling Lautréamont's prophetic injunction of "*poetry made by all*." The Hopi *Katchina* Dancers' *symbolique* achieves a synthesis of primordial rhythms, imagery, and symbolic iconography confluent with a linguistic-sonic structure collectively realized by the Masked Dancers and expresses, dynamically and visually, Hegel's definition of poetry as "the universal art." How much more satisfying is this exalting experience of collective imaginative activity, in the Hopi's peculiar synthesis of all "the arts" and rooted in a vast complex of cosmological ideas, than all the moribund mythologies and moral pretensions associated with the reified Greco-Roman classical authors.

The Hopi's vital imagery, at once magical-convulsive, became for me a veritable moving vehicle of the Poetic Marvelous, transporting me straight to those regions in the mind surrealism has always exalted. Here among a people who have retained a high degree of poetic expression in a cohesive collective form, I was made aware of a complementation of those structures, reuniting dream and concrete reality, past and present, rational and irrational, which surrealism aspires to set into free operation on the *social plane*, and suggesting analogous elements of the "new myth" surrealism has evaluated in our present civilization during the fifty years of its intrusion as a revolutionary matrix. It has become obvious that surrealism exists as a permanent means toward initiating a completely *new sensibility and civilization*, playing a role in the world communist societies of the future comparable to the festivals of living myth associated with "primitive communism" though, of course, uniquely rooted in the mythico-marvelous elements revealable in our own cultures and on another turn of the spiral of humanity's evolution through the revolutionary destruction of all alienating systems. Instead of a fragmentation of the poetic principle and suppression of its sensibility generally, as in present-day global societies, surrealism's annunciation of its *rendezvous with history* constitutes the necessity for the infinite widening of the structure of *poetry made by all* beyond its minority practice in surrealist groups, extending the concrete universality of surrealism's vital myth through which a permanent revelation of humanity shall become a *new way of life*.

Notes Toward a Rigorous Interpretation of Surrealist Occultation

Only in the moral certitude of vanquishing what resists the restoration of a blazing crown to a headless voice at the rites of permanent transgression and at the demarcation of the elected sacral site, where starlight is made to trace the initial human footprints, shall we witness the supersession of the habitual apparatus set up by external administration. Meanwhile, there remains the ongoing, permanent necessity of criticizing as well the pernicious other-side of the conformist coin constituting the many pseudo-revolts, cultural dispersals, and mystifications proliferating these days at a rate proportional to their assimilation and recuperation by the general administration. The spirit that may be permanently invoked and instigated is one of *partisan affinities* whose shields and arsenals are forged from invariable principles of liberating expression to be realized entirely on their own terms, and whose movement in the field against the superstructural obstacles must continue to be one of *implacable distance* and *distancing*, to appear as magically tempting as the Medusa, impenetrable as an interplanetary Behemoth and as resoundingly hostile to recuperation as any original violation of language.

***

Of labyrinths there are none more formidable, it seems to me, than those which *ensorcell* while extending like those "waves of snakes" whose variations multiply as one reads a mile of ancient Egyptian hieroglyphs—mazes that bewitch, I say, at the seemingly inverted pyramid whose apex reaches the heart as the sinuous path of seduction unravels, variably slow and quick, in the mind of love, in the psychic atmosphere, that is, of one who would grasp the dialectic interstices of *a moment and eternity*, each transcending the other, the horizon a steady fluidic flame, the constant quivering of desire, the "volatile" *going-over* to the "fixed" chambers about to dissolve into materialized secrets, a winged sphinx dilating whose extremities become blazing words! Actions, being-in-becoming, are explosively recognized as intrinsic to the language of "the traditional sciences," *the gesture which is transmutation*; that is, a "heightening" of immanent powers, forces, and structures. (This perspective coincidentally is worth borrowing as an "occult lever" and set afloat in that area surrealism is privileged to reveal: "a wave of dreams," the "perfect moment" of the Marvelous and toward Breton's "... of the mind in neutral gear....")

* * *

When I think of the lofty (and loftily *researched*) findings of the great philosopher Hegel as to the nature of poetic logic, its unity encompassing all the directions of human thought, and I am reminded of a few of us who have begun to practice what amounts to a collective restoration of the powers of poetic unity and as we appear, historically together intervening on the plane of American "culture" with *all the chips stacked against us*, situated against the monstrous shadow of "the new poetry" and another obscurantism of the students of those moribund minds that the false vanguards alleged to displace, I know that only armed with the living perspectives of surrealism, incarnated in *Arsenal*, am I permitted to make distinctions, draw up a relentless criticism, and inveigh against those crimes now being committed against the human spirit by mystifiers, fabricators of confusion, and all our detractors, in the certainty that my comrades and I shall not fail to be heard over and beyond, if even below, the current babble and noise of the sickening purveyors of literary and aesthetic darkness.

* * *

What is proposed ultimately and permanently: the Promethean gesture, the gesture that supersedes the cultural commodity, "the author," "the artist," "the poet," and dialectically subsumes these vain and masochistic inventions of our elders, the obnoxious enemies of desire and human freedom, who are parasitically ranged around and within us. In this pursuit we continue Rimbaud's program of the seer, who *listens* for the unheard-of, that is, the absolute becoming of what we are yet not free from, what we have yet to conquer, to supersede, namely this "tyrant" of cultural habituation, the sniveling dog of heritages, and deeper, the chattel-slave of atavism: the repressive patriarchal family structure. With Rimbaud, we must conceive of the Great Adventure as going ahead of action; we "steal fire," fire which is alchemically, psychologically, metabolically, erotically, the sole source, origin, lever, pivot—the libidinal principle itself. It is from the transformations of *libido* that desire takes wing and the cultural producer and product are essentially transcended for a phoenix-like rebirth of what shall become, of *what shall be*. Herein rest the secret correspondences, by immanent revelation, of our most profound "self" and all others; herein I discern surrealism as an organism transcending the aggregates of which it is composed; here I witness the full flowering of each individual personality by a permanent annihilation of the interior slavocracy, the becoming of that resolution; by mediations of psychical exaltations and unconditional inspiration, of the Hegelian master-slave contradiction. Otherwise I risk the mediocrity of being but another "artist" or "poet" producing what shall not bear in its secret core—but only "secret" for those who have not known the power of self-transcending desire—the flower of fire Prometheus sublimates out of his desire of desire, that is, SUBLIMES from the libidinal fire transformed by psychical powers, the highest source of conscious desire to unleash the buried treasures, so that we may pass back and forth, master of consuming and preserving fire!

Let us not forget that the Promethean pathways are uniquely *vital* as opposed to the programs of saints, contemplatives, artists, anti-artists, philosophers, and anti-philosophers, merely *outdistanced* categories for those who insist on the priorities of *the mad lover of freedom, the masterless master, and the poetic criminal!*

(To Be Continued)

1976

INVISIBLE WEBS

With the dazzling appearance of Alice Farley we are witness to a unique poetic transformation of space eliciting our affective participation in a manifestation of the profound erotism that has lain secretly coiling in the marrow of dance expression as generally understood in Western civilization. This coiled erotic force, equally exalting and convulsive if given a chance to unravel, has been repressed for countless epochs, upon which the special branding iron of Christian morality was initially applied in a crucial prohibition. This interdiction has continued to operate, albeit in our time more subtly and yet in an extremely gangrenous form, secularized as it were by rationalist barriers supporting a stifling aestheticism: from the decadent modes of Russian classical ballet to the contemporary vitiations of "modern dance." In a significant rejection of all the interdictions of a moribund aesthetic ideology as well as transcending the demoralizing effects of the anti-erotism of sterile modern dance tendencies, Alice Farley ushers into the midst of a unique event, the World Surrealist Exhibition, the fruits of years of her own singular, practical research—inspired primarily by surrealist perspectives—which opens up grand vistas of imaginary possibilities, even to a great dream of social ritual associated only with so-called "primitive" cultures in which dance is the matrix of individual-collective expression in constant revelation. Dynamically intervening with the violence of an exquisite grace, Alice Farley begins to elaborate before our eyes the three-dimensional body of movement transformed into a fourth-dimensional vessel of dreams. We can no longer remain complacently in the roles of mere spectators (as in conventional dance performances) since it is evident her dance of physical-kinetic poetry transports us to certain extreme limits, rich with excessive intensity, provoking a revolution of the senses and sparking the neural springs of our subjective being, in which suppressed desires to become "Great-Shimmering Plumage," "Winged Feet," "Delirious Volatile Head," "Fleeting Torso of the Marvelous," and any other totemical analogues of imaginary radiance, may be passionately experienced in the sense of collective interrelations summoned up by the "Prospero" within each of us, as we watch a hieratic "Alice" beckon us beyond the mirror of the alienated self, intensively on web-like feet—significantly fleeting—into an emancipatory realm of terrors, lights, and affective splendors, all the while multiplying the inferences of a "forgotten" rite regenerating within the time-durations of an expanding space of absolutely *marvelous freedom*.

1976

GEROME KAMROWSKI: THE REVELATION OF NIGHT

Gerome Kamrowski sets out on his way toward what Edward Young, a poet he invokes by correspondences, named "the narrow voyages," thereby clearing imaginary-analogical paths with the aid of a cyclopean eye (eternal instrument of seership and divination) to meet the arrival of aeroliths from outer space as they blaze a trail surprisingly lighting up a very special microcosmic heraldry. As one of his paintings ("Night Sounds") suggests, Kamrowski has achieved by his research in the treasuries of surrealist automatism the grandeurs of *revealed night*, "above as below," to paraphrase the traditional hermetic formula for exceptional discovery.

1976

RADIO VOICES:
A CHILD'S BED OF SIRENS

Activity is the faculty of receiving. —NOVALIS

Whatever its limitations, it was generally acknowledged that American radio between 1920 and 1950 had the virtue of providing a stimulating vehicle, albeit technical, for exercising a listener's imagination. Determined by radio's intrinsic structure, the listener was "forced" to "see" by responsive imaginative activity the invisible content of what is, by contrast, given and visualized in movies and television. With adults such imaginary collaboration may have been, more often than not, confined to what was directly suggested by the broadcasters, but for children up to the age of puberty certain radio dramas sparked realms of terror, desire, and reverie which infinitely improved and heightened the content far beyond the limits set rationally and consciously by the original producers. In some adventure and mystery programs of radio's so-called "golden age" (I was listening, intensively, as a child between 1934 and 1942) radioland was peopled by figures, images, and mythic concepts which served as formidable initiators of poetry and enchantment. I can trace a profound awakening of the poetic sense of life and language directly to the exemplary magical myth of *The Shadow* and to those disquieting transgressions—veritable sagas of symbolic patricide and matricide—revealed by *The Whistler*.

Among the programs aimed primarily at children, along with the science-fiction genre represented by *Buck Rogers* and *Superman*, were the realistic adventure serials: *Jack Armstrong the All-American Boy, Dick Tracy, Jungle Jim,* and *Terry and the Pirates.* Though not devoid of some spirit of risk, adventure and exoticism, the whole group was a varied expression of diurnal mentality, characteristically broadcast in the afternoon hours that followed school. Most of these daylight dramas did more or less reinforce old-fashioned ideals and morals of capitalist culture and the clichés of "law and order." But beginning in the early evening the purer mystery fantasies were featured: *Fu Manchu, Chandu the Magician, Mandrake the Magician,* and *The Shadow*. Deeper into the night, fantasy fiction came on: *Lights Out* and *The Witch's Tale,* aimed presumably at adults and adolescents, but certainly heard by the more precocious or less disciplined children, by those of us who possessed secret handmade crystal sets or managed to acquire personal bedside radios, dropping off to sleep at least once or twice a week by means of a kind of audial *Weird Tales*, the Lovecraftian pulp magazine many of us would not discover until the brink of adolescence, but for which we were being adequately prepared by radio late at night. For those who lived in the Western and Mountain areas, around nine or ten in the evening, radio on Sundays transmitted the long-running series of individual dramas linked by a basic structure fictionalizing "heinous crimes" of capitalist greed: *The Whistler. The Whistler* and *The Shadow* were conceived no doubt under the rubric of escapist adult fare, along with the detective adventure group which was also aired usually at prime time, such as the very sympathetic *Alias Jimmy Valentine* (based on O. Henry's genial safecracker) and *Boston Blackie*, both prototypes of the "good bad-guys," as well as *Bulldog Drummond*, an exotic lone-wolf from England. But what was intended by the radio producers and what occurred in a child's imaginary reception and associational development of the thematic materials from these audial sources were often contradictory—and humorously so considering the rigorously-adhered-to serious intentions of the producers and writers behind the formulas.

For children the excitement and crystallizing imagery generated through audial reception of violence, mayhem, murder, and terror far outdistanced and superseded in imaginary grandeur any possible parallels of thought and feeling an adult might have experienced. For sophisticated adults most of the radio dramas were received as variants, often banal, of the formula-fictions of the pulps; the great mass of listeners, often too tired after a hard and anxious day of work or the fatiguing anxiety of looking for work in the Depression, may not have been hearing too distinctly at all. Gilbert Seldes insisted in *The Great Audience* (1950) that radio was not, in the strict sense, a mass-media cultural form; hence, the dramas were mostly the creation of connoisseurs of certain genre-literatures who, representing a minority of the reading public, projected their special interests onto everybody, at least onto whoever was listening through the evening hours. Seldes also noted that the broadcasters were well aware of the positive effect on and high responsiveness of children to the more violent programming, so "that fifteen hundred murders take place each week on the air. This does not include murders meditated or suspected in daytime serials, but it does take in manslaughter specially arranged for children's programs."

Such shows of violence were generally salutary for children and carried for them necessary degrees of representational non-repressive sublimation, as parallel expressions in comic books and movie serials (and, long ago, fairy tales) had adequately conveyed. All the more the interventions of marvelous figures, or even merely fantastic ones, such as the Shadow, Fu Manchu, Chandu, or Mandrake the Magician, some attaining mythic dimensions, themselves transforming agents of violence and terror, transmitted audially to children, continued in new forms the unbroken line of fabulous oral literature, legend, and myth, of earlier times, where the magician such as Merlin, that counselor of vengeful battles, and the multitudinous transformations of the Shadow have served as permanent cultural motifs. If for adults the Shadow or Mandrake may be said to connote signs of regression and narcissism, for children these beings can represent truly effective symbols of triumph, power, and necessary ego-building—interacting with the child's psychic needs during the successive stages of the latency period. On the poetic plane, the Shadow and Mandrake are paragons of hermetic knowledge: modern forms, respectively, of the fairy tale wonder-worker and sorcerer. The opening theme of *The Shadow* is among the most memorable for those whose childhood games were often sparked and charged with imaginary adaptations of this potent figure. His literal visual image was known to us from two sources: graphic conceptions from the covers of the widely circulated pulp magazine devoted to him and at one juncture we were nourished by the Saturday matinee movie serial in which he was adequately portrayed by Victor Jory, who resembled, as well, some of the magazine portraits.

Psychoanalysis long ago located correspondences between practical magic and ritual in primitive societies and certain phases of our childhood psychic development. The child's psychic reality is structured in early infancy by a high sense of omnipotence continuing dynamically and transformationally through the "magical" power of words and gestures, "calling," in Geza Roheim's theory, "on all the child's sources of pleasure within its own body." Roheim wrote:

> Magic in general is the counterphobic attitude, the transition from passivity to activity ... It is probably the basic element in thought and the initial phase of activity ... We grow up through magic and in magic, and we can never outgrow the illusion of magic. Our first response to the frustrations of reality is magic; and without this belief in ourselves, in our own specific ability or magic, we cannot hold our own against the environment and against the super-ego. The infant does not know the limits of its power. It learns in time to recognize the parents as those who determine its fate, but in magic it denies this dependency. In magic, mankind is fighting for freedom ...

Simultaneously with the daytime heroines and heroes of the earliest mythology came the beings of the Night. For example, to Spaniards la Sombra (the Shadow) is to this day a familiar figure, often the name of a restaurant, café, or other popular haunt; and charmingly depicted graphically with cape and sombrero, silhouetted in black on the label of a popular wine. In folkloric investigations, Alexander Krappe found superstitious variants of the identification of "the double" or "soul" with the Shadow. By 1925 Otto Rank completed his milestone psychoanalytical study of *The Double* in which he interprets innumerable appearances and transformations of this subject from anthropological and literary sources. Maxwell Grant's pulp magazine version of 1931—perhaps inspired by Dickens and Poe—united the sense of the Shadow's earlier superstitious traditions to those of a near-omnipotent and mysterious personage with an Avenger motif; adapted for radio, the Shadow was altered to possess, as well, perhaps the most appealing of magical powers. The opening theme of the program clearly delineated both "the double" and the extraordinary power:

> The Shadow is in reality Lamont Cranston.... Several years ago in the Orient, Cranston learned a strange and mysterious secret ... the hypnotic power to cloud men's minds so they cannot see him ...

Since, during radio's golden age, children were generally trained rigorously to respect the given institutional authorities, any representation of the police as weak and ineffective as portrayed in *The Shadow* may be interpreted as an effective communication of a subversive sign, all the more enhanced by its weekly repetition. Since the depiction of police impotence was conducted within the context of comparison to an "improbable" power, the broadcasters probably rationalized the subversive quality as having been rendered diluted in a manifestly irreal form. But for children who would grow up to question or reject institutions which uphold the generalized criminality at the base of capitalist society, the subversive dimension of *The Shadow* may have been more germinal than any rationalist adult could suspect.

It is the imaginary intervention of magical power, as possessed by the Shadow and the radio magicians, among the urban landscapes of daily life which suggested the precariousness of normal social relations and hence the possibility of extraordinary transformations (here suggestions of the marvelous, but always generally intuited by humanity as rationally possible). For children who were defending themselves against the repressive demands of the parents and were capable later of questioning societal norms, great magical beings furnished the sign of a "conscience" deeper and nobler than that enforced by capitalist morality. As another mythic figure of the night, *The Vampire*, can be seen as a symbol of the latent power of the proletariat rising "from the dead" of social existence, so the Shadow becomes the Avenger of the victims of the "hidden" criminality of capitalism which has been internalized in psychical reality: "Who knows what evil lurks in the hearts of men? The Shadow knows." Though the radio producers counterbalanced the exceptional qualities of the Shadow by the use of a conventional device, i.e., enlisting him as an "aid" to "the forces of law & order," this manifest sign of accommodation was itself rendered "improbable" by the logic of the magical context in which it operated and the magical response of children nullified the device entirely. Any hypothetical rationalist or positivist "sociological" argument to the effect that the Shadow and other fantastic and mythical night-beings are reducible to mere "defenders" of capitalist law and order by the fact of adult rationalizations via mass-media ideological reinforcement, misses the point here and errs by not taking into account *the determining significance of psychical life materially interacting with socio-economic structures*. Nor with such rationalist reductionism, totally inept at understanding cultural exchanges, could there ever emerge the rich layers of latent meaning or the uncovering of inferences which signify the specific *logic of the poetic marvelous*. Any effective interventions of the marvelous impose their own logic on events, including even those fictionalized moments in crime stories which otherwise progress "realistically" but are capable of transmutation by the determinations of a magico-marvelous symbol such as *The Shadow, The Vampire, Mandrake*, or even *Chandu*! Though it has been understood in the historiography of Hollywood movies that certain filmic representations of "private-eyes"—foremost, the prototype of the "bad good-guy" or "good bad-guy" in Sam Spade of *The Maltese Falcon*—are "ambiguous" vis-à-vis established law & order, all the more the magico-mythic hero intervening in ordinary human affairs is able to turn the conventional context of cops and robbers inside out and by his superimposition of improbable means and ends implies a profound subversion of societal norms.

For an imagination highly anticipatory, such as a child's, not yet corrupted and overwhelmed by associations of routine reality, the narrations of many of radio's "opening themes," repeated ritually week after week for years, formed some of the most lasting germinal impressions emanating from popular culture. It was these thematic crystallizations that resonated with a poetic insistence and inspired irresistible moments of fervent exaltation throughout my childhood. Spells they were, auditory enchantment; talismanic voices cabalistically conveying us in vehicles structured by breathtaking excitement, irresistible affective surges of our eyes on fire beating on winged corridors of sound; waves and rivers of pulsating phonemes that swept us immediately from the first phrases into deliriums of anticipation … And as we continued to "grow up" in the remaining few years, with the underlying sense of having conquered lost ground in the passionate embrace of newly arriving landscapes emerging ever more clearly from the steamy vermilion mists, we continued almost semi-consciously to hear the radio voices of anticipation and insatiable desires for the unknown—in a great headlong rush into whatever was to be: "*invitation to the voyage,*" "*on the road to Xanadu,*" "*coming on like gangbusters.*"

The following few examples, jaded as I have become, still flicker from having once been bathed *in the first lights of glowing words*: The quoted narrations and sound-effects directions are from the opening themes of, respectively, *Lights Out, Fu Manchu, Bulldog Drummond, The Witch's Tale,* and *Boston Blackie*:

(Announcer's voice:)

"It ... is ... later ... than ... you ... think!
Lights out ...... e-v-e-r-y-b-o-d-y!"

* * *

"*London at midnight*
a great city wrapped in a heavy shroud
of dense yellow fog
... street lights weird as elfin lamps
grow mistily as something fashioned
in a dream ...

The murmur of creeping traffic. Behind an ancient wall, a vast gloomy mansion crouches like an evil beast of prey.

... The prince of evil ...
a superman of incredible genius possessing a brain like Shakespeare and a face like Satan ...
... the shadow of
Fu Manchu ..."

***

(Sound-effects:
Foghorn blasts, slow footsteps, gunshot, police whistle.)

"Out of the fog
out of the night
and into his American adventures
comes ...
BULLDOG DRUMMOND."

***

(Sound-effects:
Tower clock tolling, eerie music, howling wind.)

"The fascination for the eerie ... weird, blood-chilling tales told by Old Nancy, the Witch of Salem, and Satan, the wise black cat ..."

***

"Boston Blackie
Enemy to those who make him an enemy
Friend to those who have no friends!"

***

If in realms of a child's wish fulfillment the Shadow represented the sign-symbol of an ultimate defense mechanism, i.e., the power to appear invisible to others ("the cloak of invisibility" is a concomitant of legendary shamans, magicians, and yogis), Mandrake, who stepped into radioland from the pages of a nationally syndicated daily comic strip, was a twentieth-century interpretation of the traditional *Magus* displaying "all the powers" that have been universally ascribed to this archetype immemorially in history and myth. He was also characteristically "American." Though I imagine one could by exhaustive research find any number of "reasons why," the fact remains that the United States has *not* had in its history a mythic figure corresponding to Merlin in Britain, Faust in Germany, the historically authentic Cagliostro in eighteenth-century Revolutionary France. Cagliostro—who fascinated half of Europe, from kings and courtiers avid for his "secrets" to great masses of people who eagerly sought him out for thaumaturgic cures—was perhaps the last truly popular of the modern Great Magicians; he is doubly interesting for his anti-monarchical and subversive influence in the Freemasonic secret societies of his time, "the friend of liberty" who died in a dungeon in Italy as a victim of the Papal Inquisition.

Most fictional accounts of the modern Magus, from Bulwer-Lytton's *Zanoni*, a seminal popular novel of the Victorian age, to *Doctor Strange* in the recent comic book extravaganza, have their sources directly and indirectly in Cagliostro and his more esoteric, royalist counterpart, the Count of Saint-Germain, who also distinguished himself in the resurgence of magical belief which curiously paralleled the rationalist enlightenment and the birth of capitalism. In this latter connection, the sociologist Marcel Mauss, writing in France at the turn of the century, stated in his *Theory of Magic*, "Magical beliefs which are active in certain corners of our society and which were quite general a century ago, are the most alive, the most real indications of a state of social unrest and social consciousness..."

Though by powers and accomplishments Mandrake was easily the equal of his European counterparts, his comic-strip inventors during the Depression years chose to depict him, interestingly enough, in the guise and attire of what from the standpoint of "high magic" signifies a mere caricature of the Mage. Mandrake was drawn to look exactly like a conventional stage magician, hypnotist, or mentalist. Could it be we were confronted with another appearance of "the double," or (also implied ironically) that hard times in Depression America had forced the truly great magician Mandrake into "selling himself" in the more credible and lucrative disguise of a theatrical performer of legerdemain? But as they say here, "it worked, man," and presto—behold!—the heir of Merlin, Faust, Cagliostro, and "the great Unknown Magus" arrived in full morning or afternoon daylight replete with evening clothes, black tie, tails, short cape, tophat, and pencil-thin mustache, as if he had just finished his act from a vaudeville stage of 1920s America. Among his superior attributes he also possessed "the power to cloud men's minds," the ability to go through solid steel walls, levitate himself and others, paralyze enemies and oversee events at a distance, divert lethal objects from attaining their mark, and to cloud men's minds to the pitch of producing prodigious hallucinations to their disadvantage, etc. He even sent his seductively beautiful companion and accomplice, Princess Narda, unscathed and intact, *through a full-length mirror*.

This combinational adaptation by his inventors turned Mandrake the Magician into a veritable theatrical dandy of the occult whose stage of operations was basically the whole world of *certain interiors* of an urban landscape. He was most often depicted inside luxurious Manhattanlike apartments, fashionable restaurants, and cocktail lounges of the 1930s. And it was into *interiors* of all kinds that he invariably was drawn, as if fulfilling the old hermetic-magical invitation, in order to acquire knowledge and power, to go "into the insides of the earth." So, lo, to the extreme delight and wonder of children, Mandrake took off one day for what was to be perhaps his longest adventure; he descended into another universe, to another inhabited planet which existed in the sub-atomic spaces within the interior of an ordinary American coin! Among childhood friends and acquaintances this series of comic-strip adventures "inside the coin" was the source of endless reveries at every chance turn in the long chain of phantasmagoric events.

Though we had ample visual prefiguration of Mandrake from the comic strip, the opening theme in 1940 of the radio series had the surprising quality of an extraordinary, anticipatory annunciation. We listened to a truly oracular summons, the Latin words intoned slowly as if swept by a whirling wind and coming from a deep cave, to float over the world:

"INVOCO LEGEM MAGICORUM!"

Whether or not we understood literally the English equivalent, "*I Invoke the Law of Magic!*" these Latin sounds communicated the "cabalistic" meaning perfectly as the emblematic motto which joined to the provocative words, *Mandrake the Magician*, was instantly received as a doubly crystallized sign, an efficacious *password* to gain entry to the deepest realms of the marvelous, perfectly serving our real needs as children for the pleasures and excitement of an authentic magico-poeic experience: poetry invoked and provoked.

* * *

Gilbert Seldes also informed us that radio producers in their "golden age" deliberately aired what they considered the most violent dramas when children were apt to be listening. *Gangbusters* and the more realistic cowboys & Indians, cops & robbers, and the crime adventures were what the producers had in mind mainly, but *The Shadow, The Green Hornet, Inner Sanctum*, and a few others had their share of homicide. Many of us were listening long after "the lights" of the normal household had "gone out" and the violence, including the murders, became stranger, more gothic, and (even in adult eyes) fantastically "poetical." With the contempt reserved for children in this society, it was agreed by the cultural arbiters that the "kiddies" could be "safely" left to their own devices with the kind of *irrational* violence *The Witch's Tale* might offer.

Then, as recently, all kinds of fools parading as moralists insisted on unqualified repression of representational violence, projecting their own fears and conflicts onto children's psychical capacities. This normal reaction to sublimated and symbolical representations of violence is proportional to the rejection of the findings and insights of Freud and the psychoanalysts concerning all aspects of psychological development in infants and children. What is enraging, though, is the fact that often the moralizers who are dead set against any representational violence in the arts—specifically those of the mass media—are the staunch upholders of repressive police and military violence institutionalized in this society to reinforce its cracking structures and to repress all revolutionary action deemed a threat to capitalist power, and it is this capitalist state violence, threatening our very existence as a species, which of course must be suppressed. This stupid state of affairs, cultural and political, could not continue a moment if it were up to some of us who have reached the far points of black humor, who interrogate the night to transform the day, who see the vital necessity to reveal what goes on "in the shadows" of reality.

For the true poet, lover, and free spirit, certain cultural necessities are as primary as breathing, unless one would come to be, in any degree, at the mercy of all the diurnal "healthy-minded" worshippers of *Thanatos*, the death god, whose "trick" (similar to what Baudelaire said of the devil in the last century) might consist in hiding himself behind the very events he determines, by keeping everyone focused exclusively on the manifest content of reality, in the glare of high noon (obviously blinding)—a delusion buttressed by the general obsession with "good health" which obscures any profound sight of the festering, hidden causes of the obvious social maladies, certainly curable, of a world whose shadow and substance are held fast by the deadly and death-dealing institutions, not the least being the habitations of cultural death.

***

Since language is basically an audial system, for those in process of extending their recently acquired capacities for language-acquisition, poetic crystallizations of verbal signs received directly by the ear were complementary to the poetic and mythical expressions on the visual plane offered in some comic books and films, *e.g.*, the Saturday matinee serials: *Fu Manchu, The Shadow, Black Dragons*, and *Dr. Satan*, the latter a primitive masterpiece of the marvelous featuring one of the greatest of Hollywood actors, Eduardo Ciannelli. For me, three fertilizing rivers of popular culture—certain radio dramas, comic books, and movies—often interchanging subjects or content, were the authentic sources of poetic and life-transforming expression a child of the Depression and war years was offered, in contrast to the poverty of institutional culture, in the schools and elsewhere, whose results we would confront soon enough in the general miserabilism mercilessly enforced in adolescence and young adulthood. As in other fields, the high quantitative content of dross was immediately dissolved by certain exalting words, purified images and sounds, all the more so with radio materials which the producers deliberately structured, they believed, to last but a day and be forgotten. But as I have tried to indicate, rich thematic matter was ritually repeated and latent messages were received and often recreations of exceedingly subversive and mytho-poeic information were heard *as if for the first time*. I find little trace of poetry coming to me in childhood from any external cultural sources other than the three popular ones I have indicated. And no wonder, since elementary school rooms represented poetry, derived solely from so-called "high culture," as a hideous reduction to memorization exercises, confined to the most insipid examples of nineteenth-century versifiers, the bowdlerized versions of European balladry and fairy tales. In short, poetry in elementary schools of the United States was presented as reified and deadly by its channelization into a totally inappropriate form of mental gymnastics (memory and recitation drills). This set of cultural crimes perpetrated by the schools from childhood on contributes in no small measure, I feel, to internalizing almost insurmountable barriers to the various *forms* through which poetry seeks its end, specifically in writing but also extending to the poetic organization on the graphic and plastic planes of expression. One cannot help being reminded that we are dealing here with pedagogical practices initiating that special "hatred of the marvelous" Breton noted in the *First Surrealist Manifesto*. But every day significantly *after* school, imaginary crimes of violence were celebrated on radio with the sublime obsessive intensity of dream images, and *Mandrake*'s opening theme—"*I Invoke the Law of Magic!*"—served also as a motto for all that was most passionately responsive in the inner ears of children aspiring in identity with the mythical heroes and heroines, fulfilling absolute needs to recapture "the lost unities" and a sense of omnipotence; to respark impatience, curiosity, and unlimited capacity for imaginary life; to open the windows to the unknown, to desire more life—the key sources of all authentic poetry.

1979

THE FUTURE OF SURREALISM

BY PHILIP LAMANTIA & NANCY JOYCE PETERS

To decipher the future of surrealism is like trying to unravel the future of the Future. In short, an impossibility, a delirium. The 1970s, as everybody knows, was a sad and unnerving decade. The Left collapsed; coalitions fell apart; criticisms and condemnations blew about inchoately. The course of revolution became clouded to all but a few maniacal groupuscles. But in this dissolution/disillusion were seeds of regeneration, the stirrings of a rising phoenix.

They say the revolution failed; socialism is not possible; surrealism is dead, has been superseded. There is a monotonous regularity in these pronouncements, in them a pessimism not without an air of frenzied hope for some new panacea. Surely it is just as likely that surrealism, like viable socialism, is in an embryonic stage. It is not dead; it has yet to achieve conditions in which it can live for the first time. Like other marginal, if unresigned, territories, surrealism has been raided, colonized, robbed, distorted, marketed, misrepresented, and mystified by obscene forces of recuperation. Surrealism fails and it prevails. Whatever its "historic place," its particular triumphs or defeats, or the acts of its individual adherents, the vital impulses that have animated surrealism for over half a century are very much alive in 1981. And they continue to be inspiration, or, conversely, irritant—if nothing else a small incendiary wedge in the wretched confusions of late capitalist culture.

There is nothing original in the following summation of what endures in surrealism, as Franklin Rosemont's admirable *André Breton: What Is Surrealism? Selected Writings* attests, having made available a wealth of essential material. But these are surrealism's living currents, not confined to past, present, or unknowable future, and they bear reiterating:

1) Total commitment to human freedom and a community of equals.

2) Exaltation of Eros: the only way out of MegaDeath. Surrealism insists on the primacy of love, the myriad visions of the body, passional attraction, the satisfaction of desire. A surrealist theory of knowledge based on Eros-Made-Whole (giving weight to physical and mental perception) leads to reintegrating valuable lost qualities in man's relation to nature.

3) Subversion of positivist rituals, the cult of production, the idolatry of scientism, and imperial-bureaucratic mentality. Opposing an insanely impoverished notion of reality, surrealism, incarnating critical negation, aims to give back to humanity what has been taken away. Restoring dream, chance, passion—these are acts of augmenting, enriching, making whole. It is an inestimable misfortune that surrealism is so commonly represented as "glorifying the irrational." Worse, that media persists in using the adjective "surrealist" with criminal indiscretion.

4) Imposition of a moral imperative; the imagination of *another life* to oppose this life. In doing so, surrealism asserts that this life is unlivable

and it demands that deepest need and wildest desire be met. In a country (not yet even a social democracy) where the most minimal and mundane human requirements are ignored, these demands cry out as never before. Can surrealism be lived? Today or ever? This is beside the point. Excess, utopia, fantasy, rampage, exaggeration: These unveil a contagious image of a *marvelous living present* to be acted on, even if not yet fully.

5) Fusion of art and life. Art and poetry are not going to go away. They are not idealist aberrations to be programmed by a post-revolutionary society, nor are they, now or ever, limited to education, propaganda, or grievances in verse. They claim, always, the rebellion of the body, the insurgency of the imagination, and the potential harmony of humanity's true voice.

6) Affirmation of a unitary whole; at the same time, surrealism disintegrates structures, dissolves contradictions, and resolves paradox. The dialectic of poetic analogy. The analogic vision, the *other* voice of humankind, mediates self and other, society and the individual, the plural and unique, separation and contiguity, law and transgression, necessity and chance, humor, magic, love, and politics. Language = Poetry = Society. A radical equation: Radical Equality. In the poetic imagination, the surrealist imagination, lies the power to reveal, to transmute multifaceted reality.

1981

ALICE FARLEY:
DANCING AT LAND'S END

And it is a dream at sea such as was never dreamt, and it is the Sea in us that will dream it:

The Sea, woven in us, to the last weaving of its tangled night, the Sea, in us, weaving its great hours of light and its great trails of darkness—
——ST.-JOHN PERSE, *Seamarks*

I want a revolution in which the dream is realized in space. The revelation of this possibility took material shape in those exalting moments of poetic history when I watched Alice Farley draw forth, in broad daylight, those strands of becoming whose invisible sources lie within us, to be revealed on the oneiric screen of our lives. Lautréamont's "Old ocean..." was evoked in a vibrant transmutation of space bestowed by Alice in her "commingling" with the fragile spirits of poetry at the extremes of convulsive desire through, in her own words, "... the subversion of the physical laws of gravity, momentum, inertia, by imagination and desire...." On the precipitous rocks of cliffs overlooking mineral excrescences from who knows what depths of some primordial dialectics of sea and earth, mist and light, and in which inner rages were confounded with the turmoil of the breakers below—not far from Frisco's "golden gates"—a new being was born whose timelessness transcends all the miseries of the world. We have seen the "Woman in Tree" and the "Wheel of the Lovers" in the *androgynies* Farley has materialized in paths of flight and bathed in purifications of our senses made possible by the sublimity of *The-Marvelous-in-Motion*. At those origins in the mysterious waters in which we ourselves are conveyed, the living myth of the ultimate west has been danced in photonic revelation, along those threads uniting the double strands of sleep and waking. Here in the oneiric matrix of "the waters of the west," where birth and death are one, and from the other side of the looking glass, dance has been irrevocably raised forever to the power of poetry.

Alice Farley is one of today's most innovative and brilliant young dancers and choreographers. Her originality lies in masterful kinesthetic fusions of the dancer's grace and skill with a world-range of musics, costumes, and masks, through which she creates a domain of moving images like those in surrealist painting and poetry. Landscapes—from New York City streets to Paolo Soleri's model desert city to San Francisco's ocean shore—can never be seen in the same way again, once touched by the enchantment of Alice Farley's dance. Among her major performances are: Fortunate Light, *San Francisco, 1974;* The Brides of the Prism, *San Francisco, 1975;* Surrealist Dance, *Chicago World Surrealist Exhibition, 1976;* (In)Visible Woman, *New York City, 1977;* Land's End, *San Francisco, 1978; and* The Atomic Thief in the Circus of Crime, *New York City, 1981. Alice Farley is affiliated with the Theater for the New City and is a member artist of Dance Theater Workshop, 219 West 19th Street, New York City 10011.*

1982

MARIE WILSON

Marie Wilson's heraldic neighborhood of "the king of the world" in his spectral aspect—Night (the crocodile-river-run to wings of delphic daemons) situates its cotidian mask, or sets of masks, on the interior crags where the "spirits of the woods" empty cosmological windows of their last specks of dust, and, lo, we've flown free to the golden coffers at this far western site.

January 1984

CLARK ASHTON SMITH PLAQUE DEDICATION

This is the third time I have visited Auburn. All three trips have been literary trips, and all connected with Clark Ashton Smith. In 1978, my wife Nancy and I stopped here to look at the library holdings of Smith's books of poetry—with a tentative idea to reissue a chapbook edition, so that his poems might be made available again. And then a few years ago, we were taken on a splendid tour of the "Bard of Auburn's" homes and haunts by Donald Sydney-Fryer who, as many of you here may know, addressed his considerable energies to a bio-bibliography of *The Emperor of Dreams*. At that time, as we talked in the field where Smith's cabin once stood, we hoped the state of California would establish a park there to commemorate the exceptional achievement of her native son. Today it is an honor to be in Auburn once again to be a part of these ceremonies to dedicate a memorial plaque as a tribute to him.

Clark Ashton Smith had a unique combination of gifts: an inordinate love of the language, of words themselves, a daring speculative mind, and a poetic imagination that informed us of a vast network of parallel worlds, what certain twelfth-century Sufis called "the third world of images," analogous to the tales of the *Arabian Nights* which were one of the inspirations of Smith's youth. Those Sufi authors envisioned the concrete world of our psycho-sensorial field, that of the ineffable, and of the *mundus imaginalis*, that is, the Imaginary World—a third world of images which can be explored and revealed, as it was by Smith's imagination.

In one of the earliest literary tributes to Smith, the critic Robert Allerton Parker noted, in 1942, the "bitter black humor" which threads through Smith's science fiction. At the same time, the author transmutes the material of science and fantasy in his tales and poems so that they become "imaginative and humorous allegories of human aspirations." (This recalls the poet's affinity with another genius associated with Auburn: Ambrose Bierce.) The twin threads of transformational imagination and black humor are sources that link Smith, as well, to the irrepressible gnostic "other side" of the last two thousand years. Since Smith's time, this current has been amply perceived in the hundred rediscovered texts of gnostic imagination, the domain of Ialdabaoth, a tradition of the Marvelous with its attendant terror and joy, sudden awakenings, and deep dreams—all that of the flying, transcendent death. All this is invoked by our poet. Although the literary mainstream, blinded by an unbalanced "realism," denied it, I am happy to say that Smith followed his poetic genius to reveal the heights and depths of a rich cosmic reverie.

I have become, over the years, ever more intrigued with the way in which Northern California has been embodied in the works of its writers and poets. While Steinbeck's Monterey, or Twain's Gold Country, or Hammett's

San Francisco give us a sense of time, of an historical era with its customs and characters, Smith gives us a timeless land, a feeling for the form of the earth, the Pacific, the oak-covered knolls of the Coast Range, the fog-shrouded tip of the San Francisco peninsula, the huge skies and sunsets, the Sierra Nevada's rustling foothills.

His paraworlds, such as *Zothique*, not only remind us of the vast span of cosmic time and put our own culture into a temporal perspective, but they capture a complex spirit of place. Auburn was once the site of three Maidu Indian villages. The first people knew the spirits of the land, and after becoming familiar with their myths, one can never travel this country without feeling the presence of Coyote, Blue-Sided Lizard, or the Stone People. The same is true of Smith. In quite the same way, but with a macabre and ironic sensibility appropriate to our own time, he irrevocably changed the way we experience this region. We're aware of possible dark terrors beyond the nearby hill, feel a thrill of expectancy as we round the next bend in the road. What sorceries or infernos might open for us? Might we pass through the Boulder gate in the Sierra to the *City of the Singing Flame*? If lucky, we'll escape Smith's gnostic telos and not be cast back into this imperfect state. We could enter another dimension, or find a way to create an alternative world right here.

Gustav Meyrink, a near-contemporary of Smith, and best known in English for *The Golem*, wrote of humanity's fear of the supernatural, against which it has built "a wall of materialism.... This wall is an infallible protection; it is an image of the physical body, but at the same time also a prison wall that blocks the view...." By his imaginary life, I believe Clark

Ashton Smith quite literally dwelt in this view of another reality behind appearances, so much against the grain of his time that now I can see him clearly as a great harbinger. Black-humorist, visionary, poet, and seer: a man to change consciousness.

Auburn, California
August 18, 1985

STATEMENT ON "HOWL"

1953, Spring, aged 25, reading the Koran on a couch, one night, I was suddenly physically laid out by a powerful force beyond my volition, which rendered me almost comatose: suddenly, consciousness was contracted to a single point at the top of my head through which I was "siphoned" beyond the room, space, and time into *another* state of awareness that seemed utterly beyond any other state before or since experienced. I floated toward an endless-looking universe of misty, lighted color forms: green, red, blue, and silver, which circulated before me accompanied by such bliss that the one dominant thought was: This is it; I never want to return to anywhere but this *place*—i.e., I wanted to remain in this Ineffable Blissful Realm and explore it forever—since I felt a radiance beyond even further within it and so, suddenly the outline of a benign bearded Face appeared to whom I addressed my desire to remain in this marvel—and who calmly replied: "You can return, after you complete your work."

May 25, 1986
New Orleans

LETTER FROM EGYPT

November 1, 1989

[Sat, Nov 22, '89]

Dear André & Goldian—Well, perhaps, the *less* one stays in Cairo the better, though we've had seven days and nights viewing a splendid part of it from a six-floor terrace-balcon overlooking the *Hapy*. Charmed to see, for a pleasant example, fishermen outlined in their simple, tiny boats in *Amenti*, catching up their nets in the old ways. On the negative side (only apparent *after* I'd sent you the initial post-card of our first day here—hope you got it?—) the attempt to cross even the arterial six streets off the chaos of traffic in Tahrir Square brought me within minutes to unprecedented stress and to possibility of nerve damage, if not "break-down," i.e., "paranoic anxiety" hard to describe! Poor Nancy had to put up with hysteric me, though she remained relatively calm, by far, in the face of this horrendous car scene & carbon-monoxide horror that is characteristic of the general state of this city she had remembered 25 years ago as being friendly, overly polite, non-alienated and, relatively, serene with a population of a million or two instead of the *twenty* million now on each average day! (The nights are reputed to contain *only* 15 million.) Food is pretty good, though, and I detect in the cuisine the origin of much Mediterranean cooking, Italian, Provençal, Catalan, etc.—eggplants in several forms, fava beans (*foul*) and the good unleavened bread. Also, the *Cleopatra* cigarette tobacco may explain de Lubicz's permanent habit; there's really no better, easily available kind. Now, I'm nearing about a pack a day after four years of abstinence—though this delight terminates at the Cairo Airport come November 17th!

Thoughts after arriving at Luxor, 11.1.89: onto, and inclusive of, 12 days in Luxor

We arrived to greet the dawn from our wagon-lit compartment with four-hour vistas moving off the green fellaheen fields of lush gardens & scattered habitations ... and yes, there were hundreds of cattle egrets. Persons emerged in rustic galabeyas from non-electrified brick houses, and carrying ancient hoes; it could have been a scene from the 18th Dynasty. Here is a place the natural vegetable cultivation accounts for the renewed vitality we almost immediately noticed, even in Cairo, or now, in Luxor, waking up completely at pre-dawn to hear a thousand sparrows in our lovely garden room of this antique hotel just a few yards, also, from the Nile. Here we have the constant vista, though, of the Theban Hills outlined on the western horizon above the Valley of the Kings and Queen H[atshepsut]'s great temple.

[few days later]

Now, I'm about to begin—with a profound sense of grandeur—to thread the edges of a realm "hazy," indeed, for literate reflection: perhaps, only schematic descriptiveness can invoke it. Yet, André, your, no doubt, greater familiarity might bridge the gap to my poor renditions to follow, though I hardly am thinking of little else last few days. I might even hazard the guess that you, Goldian—having remembered your recent communications re the architectonics of the Cathedral—may also feel something of what Nancy & I have shared traversing *The Temple of Man*, subsequent to the twenty-five-year read in the Schwallerian text. Here goes, folks—I hope you'll pardon the inevitable digressions and the jumble of expressions. However, it all seems fairly clear to me now, as in those radiant moments of exalted discovery.

Morning: *2nd day in Luxor Temple*:

There are few "tourists" when we arrive about seven—with our two "guide" books: *The Temple of Man* and *Sacred Science*. Few months ago, in my Frisco study, I'd begun to interest myself in Rooms 12 & 20 of the Covered Temple and copies of our books with us now contain marginal notes, underlined parts I'm anxious to review on the site. We buy the fifty-cent tickets at the sleepy gatekeepers' entrance (incidentally, the tickets resemble the very ones you collaged for *Al-Kemi*'s cover). We face the two great Pylons—before entering the Narthex—we re-read all the material on the Battle of Kadesh—Then with poised Leitz and Swarovski binoculars begin to survey first the west and east pylons; we find on the east pylon, near the top, the King in Chariot bordered by Nine Bows. Re-checking the references on pg. 98 in *The Temple of Man*, I notice de Lubicz's indication of the important correspondence to Room 12. Hence begins our initial *trajectory* through the T.—going straight from the reading of Kadesh on the outer walls of the Great Pylons to the Covered T. This is and remains the most significant *action* since it is of an entirely different order than the usual conventional logic of advancing to view the walls of the successive enclosures: only with the textual fruits of de Lubicz's work is this marvelous trajectory possible for the likes of us! This gives the form to what I meant by "discovery"—Once we meditate the glyphic representations in Room 12, we both begin, simultaneously, to experience that extraordinary state of Recognition which gives an exceptional qualitative character to this Temple: here, too, is where what we see and understand borders the "mystical"—if it were not for the geometric sense of what has happened in thought, in consciousness via de Lubicz. It's a vision of the confondement of rational and irrational, alright—specifically, the rationally graspable geometric correspondence between the historical support—the Battle of Kadesh on the pylons *and* the *medulla oblongata* of the human brain! Now we begin to really appreciate the unbridgeable gap dividing academic Egyptology and inner knowledge of the supreme representation of the SACRED SCIENCE. It seems to me the first specific *clear* revelation of a kind of *traversal-reflex*. (A: is this not a plausible technical term worth using?) And so, "extra-muros," later, I reflect that I've touched "base," again, with what I had grasped long ago with you at Heliopolis. Further reviews of the texts and subsequent encounters on our *third* visit to the Temple Luxor reconfirm the link between Heliopolis and the Theban Mystery, further enhanced by our first visit in the Temple of Karnak the next day, meditating, from text, glyphs, and repetitions on the walls concerning the triad of *Amon*, *Mut*, and *Khonsu*. This latter understanding bringing us straight to consideration of the Memphite mystery as is evident in Karnak—indeed with *The Sacred Science* volume we were directed quickly to the main representations of "the central theme" and got the message of the "grand synthesis." (I remember, excitedly, the 2 vols. awaiting me in Frisco of *The T.K.*—a lifetime—or many lifetimes?—to *de-fine it*!) Again, we haven't examined many of the glyphic representations of *Neter* on other walls of this truly immense Stone Book, but continue following a cycle of Theban Triads throughout it. Here, also, is the specific Pharaonic way located visually and physically by us that seems a clear pre-figuration of the Christic Mythos with an expansive consciousness founded, thanks to the Master, to an ever-deepening clarity of *entendement*. O.K.

Temple of *Karnak*

Second revelation in front of bas-relief of *Sed Festival* on the west wall. (*Sacred Science*, pg. 240–247)—

Here we are provoked to consider the whole destiny of Man and each of us, at once, from the angle of the *KA* and the higher Ka, possibility and necessity, for some, of coming into the trajectory of a supra-human *telos*. All this is grasped with another instance of expanding consciousness focused by crystal clear comprehension and in recognition of what Pharaonic Egypt achieved to *transmit* to us reading its messages, *now*. I more deeply understand—no matter how disgusted with the "group tours" at the sites, the State's mismanagement, and the mediocrity of "modern" Egypt—how important it was for N and I to be here—as I said on the phone to you, strangely "summoned" here. Nancy and I reach perfect, true—"four times" true—*harmony* of being, thought: the fruit of love is affinity: the fullness of presence, of present moment: *twenty-five years in the making of it*!

Summary from the Diagonal Trajectory in the Temple of Luxor:

It occurs to me that though our personal way of traversing the Temple is *implied* by the correspondences given by our Master-Guide-Author, our *individualized* way of actually, physically, & consciously *doing it*, invoked a meditation on specific modes of *the personal ka's*. And, all the more amazing, to have realized the fact that our movements in space corresponded at crucial moments with a diagonal trajectory, e.g., from "*N*" at the western corner of the Peristyle Hall *to* Room Twenty in the Covered Temple. The Golden Section has come alive-in-thought for me—expansively and with amazing clarity—realigning my awareness to the seeds of consciousness experienced at Heliopolis! Now, I will return to the Frisco work space and really—with this newly gained clarity—attempt an extension of geometric thought with the promise of a certain sense of "diligence"—practical diligence, that is, I once lacked.

Again in Cairo—Nov 14-16.1989:

Now to close this epistle, except to mention, briefly, impressions in the last two days around Luxor when we got over the River Nile to visit one of the Tombs of the Kings, namely Ramses VI. There upon entering a brightly lit interior disclosing a fresh ensemble of wall paintings that we—hairs literally standing, electrically charged—beheld what is for vision the *tomb of a living king*! The vibrant colors—reds, blues, whites, gold—are in my mind's eye forever. We both understood de Lubicz's insistent perception of the Egyptian Gesture as it relates to LIFE, HEALTH, STRENGTH revealed on the aesthetic plane, at once, with the philosophic. We were, at last, tangibly in the presence of the Living Face of Pharaonic Egypt. After descending about (or more than) a hundred feet into the tomb at the sight of the paintings on ceiling and walls of the Sarcophagus chamber at the end, I couldn't help saying to N: "This tomb contains the greatest paintings I've ever seen." Yes, the vital quality of such paintings, the simple-complex structure of their execution reveals an aesthetic mystery of highest excellence & perfection which even the finest reproductions *never* convey. If for nothing else, one's physical presence in Egypt opened us to this unique Reception, a "gift" which complements the geometric & philosophic insights traversing the Temples of Luxor and Karnak (we also went to Medinet-Habu).

Whatever—: relative directions being unequal in manifestation (individual differentiations of inner necessities—) I am ultimately happy & grateful to have come to be fed so sumptuously for my own Ka's sake—whereas I believe you, *two*, are probably already so richly endowed—having shared a year with de Lubicz when you started in *Kemi*—that your physical journey here to the SITES would give you no more than the *second* helping of your favorite dessert!

See you!

Philip

Love to you,

Nancy

PREFACE TO <u>CROSSROADS OF THE OTHER</u> (1992) BY KEN WAINIO

It is not at all apparent where the "volcanic summit" in one of Ken Wainio's poems, "Ventriloquist," may actually be located in the physical world. True, his poetic space manifests land, sea, moon and starry scapes, marked, sustained and transformed by constant reverie and practiced attention to, and interaction with, an evidently fertile dream life. Nevertheless, it so happens this oneiric space perfectly complements his native and childhood haunts in the environs of Redwood Valley, a relatively pristine inland region a hundred miles almost due north of San Francisco. This is Pomo Indian country through which the Russian River flows, alternately life-sustaining or turbulent from pelting rains. This river was once lined with numerous villages of Pomo-speaking tribelets whose other discontinuous territories were spread north and east of the river, including the once idyllic region surrounding Clear Lake, the largest wholly within California. Risen from a nearby plain, overlooking the lake, is solitary Mount Konocti, whose name means Female Mountain, to this day covered by the bodily remains of the Herculean, supernatural being of Pomo myth, Obsidian Man, whose hard glassy black & brown parts are encountered strewn everywhere at the base of this once volcanic mountain.

This present collection belongs to Wainio's first decade or so of living in San Francisco, where apparently viable contact was made with a few of us attempting an extension of poetic surrealism. The three-part prose poem, "Letters from Rimbaud," is also a touchstone carrying an anticipatory sign of "a new country" that may await those whose "footsteps are seeds." Such interior journeys foreshadowed Wainio's season in Egypt (1979), which inspired his first published book of prose, *Letters from Al-Kemi*, a high-spirited travelogue, studded with his peculiar sense of humor, which also delineates a plausible self-portrait and whose opening sentence corresponds to what is most singular in his poetry. "It is true I have always felt a strong attraction to Ancient Egypt, her people and art, as if I possessed an innate race memory of that vanished culture, or found personal evidence in my reveries for the transmigration of souls."

Of poets who wrote in the English language it seems significant to mention certain central theoretical ideas that anticipated the surrealist project for poetry. Shelley with enthusiastic approval cites Milton's principle that his muse "dictated" to him "the unpremeditated song." Poe held in the highest estimation those involuntary images, "fancies" he called them, which rise from within us in privileged moments "between wakefulness and sleep." The very title, *Crossroads of the Other*, suggests that the poet has found the way to mediate composition, to paraphrase André Breton, from "communicating vessels" of unconscious sources of inspiration and conscious activity. This fertilizing relation, of conscious and unconscious mental perception, is the sole structure that allows the liberation of eroticized energy as a basic force field to determine a living poetic text in contradistinction to the passionless and contrived elucubrations of false poets. Erotic presence turns into poetic evidence. For Wainio the erotic-marvelous arrives on dove's feet, branded with suffering, clear-obscure, even, yet flashing redolent sparks and finally erupts highly condensed in the superb poem "Driving Through Mexico," celebrating a double victory of the road's freedom with animating fires lighting up the green source of eternal recurrence. Apposite to the erotic-marvelous, objective humor also erupts, by turns fantastic and absurd, as in "Bourgeoisie," subverting by a healthy misanthropy the hidden demonology of misdirected global societies of fragmented victims ("the living dead") that survive their decadence by ever more violent means—ecocide and nuclear threat—and through isolation of whatever exists of a tiny minority of beings attempting reintegration and resurrection of real life a true poet announced not too long ago, "is absent."

PROGRAM NOTE FROM A READING AT THE POETRY PROJECT AT ST. MARK'S CHURCH, APRIL 1999

Born San Francisco 1927. Inspired contact with surrealism in 1943 during the month-long retrospectives of Dalí and Miró at the local museum. Finds some theoretic writings by Breton and begins writing from the zone of "pure psychic automatism." Discovers *View: A Magazine of the Arts* (edited by C. H. Ford and Parker Tyler) who instantly accept five poems featured in the June 1943 issue. Not long after (having found the "official" surrealist review edited by André Breton, Duchamp, Ernst, and David Hare) at the request of Breton clarified his position about surrealism in a letter titled "Surrealism in 1943," which was published along with a page of poems in the 4th and last number of the review *VVV*. 1944: lived in New York City where he met with Breton and other surrealists-in-exile, along with artists in affinity with the movement such as Maya Deren, Kurt Seligmann, Lionel Abel, Harold Rosenberg, and Charles Duits whose hospitality he enjoyed frequently during this sojourn. Also in Manhattan, deepened his appreciation of the new jazz currents heard in nightclubs of that era.

Returned to San Francisco by 1945. Edited first number of *The Ark*, a new magazine reflective of the post–World War II anarcho-pacifist culture he was part of, along with Kenneth Rexroth and other poet-friends later identified as the "San Francisco Renaissance." Published first book, *Erotic Poems*, 1946. In 1950 moved again to New York City where he first met and hung out with Allen Ginsberg, Jack Kerouac, and Carl Solomon, etc.

Living in Mexico from remote regions of the Cora Indians in the mountains of the Western Sierra, San Blas to Mexico City, during various periods in the 1950s and early 1960s. Published *Ekstasis*, 1959, and *Destroyed Works*, 1962. 1963: went on a five-year odyssey to Spain, Morocco, France, and Greece. Early surrealist poetry collected and published as *Touch of the Marvelous*, 1966; first City Lights book, *Selected Poems*, 1967. Initial and abiding contact with the Western esoteric tradition through André VandenBroeck who, not long before the death of, in 1966, studied almost daily for two years with R. A. Schwaller de Lubicz, whose monumental work, *The Temple of Man*, is at last translated from the French into English, published in 1998 by Inner Traditions. Lamantia's longish poem, "Egypt," dedicated to Schwaller, is the second to last poem in *Bed of Sphinxes* (City Lights Books, 1997).

Since 1970, Lamantia has been living in San Francisco where he has taught at SF State and SF Art Institute various times; subsequent books: *Blood of the Air* (1970), *Becoming Visible* (1981), *Meadowlark West* (1986), and most recent, *Bed of Sphinxes: New and Selected Poems 1943–1993*.

Frequent travels and sojourns in Northern California's wilder regions and AmerIndian sites inspired a poetry that re-imagines natural forms from the inner zone surrealism located "between sleep and waking" Poe was the first to specify.

SURREALISM & MYSTICISM

RESPONSES FROM A LAST INTERVIEW

Lamantia: There have been times when I considered my relationship with surrealism over. When I returned to SF in the late '40s, my poetry underwent a complete 360° turn, under the influence of Rexroth. I wanted to write more "naturalistic" verse, very little of which I ended up keeping.

What about the mystical poems of Ekstasis*?*

I wrote much of *Ekstasis* during my initial conversion to Catholicism, in the early '50s, though I eventually drifted away from the Church. I didn't quite have the philosophical sophistication I have now, in terms of understanding mysticism. By "mystic," I mean the experience of having something previously unknown reveal itself to you, a direct communication with God. One in which you feel God's love in an ecstatic, physical way.

Is the mystic equatable with the marvelous?

In *Ekstasis*, I wrote "Christ IS the marvellous!" so yes, I felt a continuity between surrealism and mysticism. I believe that erotic love and spiritual love are essentially the same. Take the word "passion"; it indicates both the saint's experience of God and the lover's experience of the beloved, and with good reason. The use of the same term shows people knew this at one point, but it's been forgotten.

How does surrealism, or poetry more generally, relate to this conception of the erotic?

In *Mad Love*, Breton said he had no interest in any art that didn't produce the same "shiver" in him the erotic did. This is what I'm talking about. Except that I equate poetry and eros with the mystical experience. I imagine this isn't a popular attitude today, but I think it adequately describes the type of thing I'd call "poetry." Much of what passes as poetry today I have no interest in, whether it's automatic writing or collaged from a newspaper. Both activities were important parts of surrealism, but they're outmoded, at least at the moment. If the poem is not written in a state of passion—what we used to call THE ZONE—then forget it.

So what is the major difference for you between surrealism and Catholicism?

As you know, Breton despised the Catholic Church. He was an atheist-materialist. Yet he often was "accused" of being a mystic, and he did evoke "the spirit" in his political and poetic discussions, so much so that several Catholic intellectuals found surrealism's aspirations identical to their own. They equated God with the marvelous, as I did in *Ekstasis*. Also, in the '50s, when it came out that Michel Carrouges, who Breton claimed wrote the best book on surrealism, was actually a Catholic, it led to one of the biggest rifts in the movement. Several younger members left, because Breton was reluctant to throw Carrouges out. But the fact is that orthodox surrealism does reject Catholicism as such.

While I officially reembraced surrealism in 1970, and almost exclusively appeared in surrealist controlled publications, already by 1982, I no longer considered myself an "orthodox" surrealist in any way. When I wrote the poems collected as *Meadowlark West* in 1986, poetic surrealism served as only one element.

Is there now no contradiction between surrealism and Catholicism?

I find no contradiction. But you have to understand that there are still plenty of orthodox surrealists out there who'd disagree. Perhaps you could call me a "mystic surrealist," if anyone would understand that, since both words have been corrupted. One thing people miss about surrealism is that it evolves, even as it stays the same; Breton said as much, considering it something that predated his discovery and yet adapted to the times. It's the same with the church. It changes but remains unchanged in essence. My sympathies are with the innovative yet traditional side of the Church, the mystical tradition that's often been overlooked or forgotten.

What is the role of poetry in contemporary culture?

Like mysticism, poetry aims to reveal what is unknown to us, but also to make us conscious of what is already inside us. This is what Plato meant by "unconscious knowledge"; the "unconscious" wasn't a psychological concept for him but a matter of knowledge that had yet to be revealed. Surrealism, having thrown open the relation between the unconscious and the conscious now for me germinates the seed of the "surconscious." This is a third term in a triadic structure of thought, as articulated by Wolfgang Paalen, where unconscious and conscious cease to be contradictions. We live now in a state of idol worship of a science enslaved by technology, despite the insistence of scientists from Paracelsus to Einstein on the central role of inspiration in their work.

2001

STATEMENT

As with Poe and Milton, passion is qualified as the central sun of poetry—indeed, analogously, the human and suprahuman erotic, the active and creative principle, attains infinite degrees of transformational power. Poetry has yet to recover its function as a conductor/vehicle of essential knowledge (gnosis). Passionate love is the lever for the poet *and* saint; androgynous union: source and culmination in renewal of vital energy.

Designated "The Magnificent" by André Breton, the symbolist poet Saint-Pol-Roux reminds us: "Poetry is nothing less than the renewal of God's original activity." It is a traditional saying (hermetic): "The root of heaven is on earth." Saint Catherine of Siena: "Desire is infinite." By analogy to the above triad, I suggest "The past is in the future." Furthermore, mystery illuminates the marvelous in all things and surreality inhabits the marvelous mystery at the core of all and any reality.

—*P.L. (July 24, 2001)*

BIBLIOGRAPHY

BY STEVEN FAMA

Letter to Charles Henri Ford

1943. Published here for the first time. Several years ago, an unauthorized color photocopy of Lamantia's signed, two-page, typewritten letter was briefly offered for sale online.

An edited version of the letter's third-to-last paragraph, under the title "Surrealism and the Unconscious," was published in the letters-to-the-editor section of *View*, Series III, No. 2 (June 1943: New York), page 65. As stated in the introduction, this issue of *View* also included five poems by Lamantia—"I Am Coming," "Apparition of Charles Baudelaire," "The Ruins," "By the Curtain of Architecture," and "There Are Many Pathways to the Garden"—his first appearance in print aside from a single poem in a California high school anthology. See Garrett Caples, Andrew Joron, and Nancy Joyce Peters, *The Collected Poems of Philip Lamantia* (Berkeley: University of California Press, 2013) (hereafter *CPL*) at pages xxv–xxvii and 6–8.

Surrealism in 1943

VVV, No. 4 (February 1944: New York), page 18.

A photograph of Lamantia, in the style of a yearbook portrait, appears at the top right of the page on which his statement/letter is printed. The photo was later used on the cover of *Touch of the Marvelous* (Berkeley: Oyez, 1966) and has been published elsewhere. (See, e.g., *CPL* at page xxviii.)

Three of Lamantia's poems are printed on the page across from his prose: "The Islands of Africa," "Touch of the Marvelous," and "Plumage of Recognition." See *CPL* at pages xxvii and 3–5.

The Tchelitchew Cover

View, Series IV, No. 1 (Spring [March] 1944: New York), page 23.

The painting commented upon appeared on the cover of the previous issue of *View*, Series III, No. 4 (December 1943).

Young Poets

View, Series V, No. 1 (March 1945: New York), pages 50–51.

Largely devoted to writings about Marcel Duchamp and his work, this issue of *View* features covers by the artist and a center foldout, die-cut triptych on which he collaborated. The issue was also produced in a specially bound edition of 100 copies, each signed by 18 of the contributors (not including Lamantia, who had returned to San Francisco by the time the issue was published), with each having a reproduction of Duchamp's *Pharmacy* (1914), hand-colored, numbered, dated, and signed by the artist.

An American Opinion

Freedom Through Anarchism (London, England: November 3, 1945), page 2.

Lamantia's first publication outside the United States. This twice-monthly anarchist paper was edited by George Woodcock.

More than 60 years after publication, Lamantia emphasized to this bibliographer that John Hershey's *Hiroshima*, published in the *New Yorker* on August 31, 1946, then later that same year as a book by Alfred A. Knopf, was an important text regarding The Bomb.

Conscientious Objector's Statement

1945. Published here for the first time. Manuscript in Philip Lamantia Papers, 1944–2005, Bancroft Library, University of California, Berkeley [BANC MSS 2006/179].

Letter from San Francisco

Horizon, No. 93–94 [double issue] (October, 1947: London), pages 118–123.

Reprinted as *Letter from San Francisco* (Coventry, England: Beat Scene Press, 2009).

Editorial from The Ark *(1947)*

The Ark (Spring 1947: San Francisco), n.p. [3–4].

The editorial is not signed. Nor are the editors named in the table of contents or elsewhere in the magazine.

Conscientious Objector's Statement II

1949. Published here for the first time. Manuscript in Philip Lamantia Papers, 1944–2005, Bancroft Library, University of California, Berkeley [BANC MSS 2006/179].

Two Introductions to John Hoffman

Lamantia, Philip, *Tau*; with *Journey to the End* by John Hoffman. Edited by Garrett Caples (San Francisco: City Lights Books, 2008), pages 71–78.

The first of the introductions (1954) appears in *Journey to the End* ([San Francisco]: Bern Porter, 1956), an announced but never published book which appears to exist only in a one-off bound edition with "diazo process reproductions of typescript, illustrations, and handwriting," in the special collections library at the University of California, Los Angeles (Call Number: PS3515.H676j). The second introduction was written in 1959.

Hymns to St. Geryon *(1959) by Michael McClure*

The Auerhahn Press [1959].

A catalog and publicity sheet for the press's publications, formatted as a four-panel 20″ × 5.5″ folded broadside, tipped into fold-over covers. Paragraphs are indicated by a kind of double quarter-moon printer's mark, italics by orange instead of black text.

Biographical Note in The New American Poetry, 1945–1960

Allen, Donald M., editor, *The New American Poetry, 1945–1960* (New York: Grove Press, 1960), page 440.

Vision and Instigation of Mescaline 1961

Published here for the first time. Manuscript in Philip Lamantia Papers, 1944–2005, Bancroft Library, University of California, Berkeley [BANC MSS 2006/179].

The word "mescaline" appears once in Lamantia's poetry, in the late 1990s poem "Hyper-Sleep." *CPL* at pages 425–426 ("hallucinating on *the other side /* greater than any mescaline-visioned sky …").

The Beat Generation

1961. Published here for the first time. Manuscript in Philip Lamantia Papers, 1944–2005, Bancroft Library, University of California, Berkeley [BANC MSS 2006/179].

Lamantia's reference here to "the sculpture of Bruce Conner" brings to mind that the two had met each other in the late 1950s, a few years before this text was written, and that in October 1961, Lamantia, who had been living in Mexico City for some time, helped Conner and his wife Jean find a place to live when those two moved there. See Rachel Federman, "Bruce Conner: 50 Years in Show Business," in Rudolf Frieling and Gary Garrels, editors, *Bruce Conner: It's All True* (Berkeley: University of California Press, 2016) at pages 31 and 83. In 1962, a photograph of Conner's SUPERHUMAN DEVOTION (1960) assemblage was used on the cover of Lamantia's *Destroyed Works* (Auerhahn Press, 1962). Many years later, Lamantia presented the artist a copy of *Becoming Visible* (San Francisco: City Lights, 1981) in which he had inscribed, "To Bruce Conner / who *is* visible / in Buster Keaton."

Mental Cement

1964. Published here for the first time. Manuscript in Philip Lamantia Papers, 1944–2005, Bancroft Library, University of California, Berkeley [BANC MSS 2006/179].

RevelatNewsPort by Raphael Kohler

1964. *International Times [IT]*, No. 38 (London: August 23–September 5, 1968), page 3.

Reprinted without illustrations in Mairowitz, David, editor, *Some of IT* (London: Knullar, 1969) at pages 143–145.

The issue and essay as first published is available online at http://www.internationaltimes.it/archive/index.php?year=1968&volume=IT-Volume-1&issue=38&item=IT_1968-08-23_B-IT-Volume-1_Iss-38_003 (accessed August 19, 2017).

Launched in late 1966, the English counterculture newspaper *International Times* appeared fortnightly for several years thereafter. The title of Lamantia's essay appears at the very top of the paper's front sheet, and serves as the issue's lead article. An editor's note at the top right of page 2 explains that Raphael Kohler is a pseudonym for Lamantia, and provides a brief biography. The essay itself, along with reproductions of two unattributed drawings, takes up the entire 12″ × 18″ four-columned page on which it appears. The drawings, while seemingly not referencing matters or scenes described in the essay, mirror Lamantia's wild energy. The larger of the two drawings depicts, among other things, a supine, perhaps dead Santa Claus whose chest has been impaled by the bottom of a burning wooden cross upon which a crucified Mickey-Mouse-headed mermaid has been stuck in the chest by a large syringe while a mustachioed English bobby, wearing the customary buttoned-up uniform and custodian helmet, calmly tickets the entire scene.

Notes Towards a Poetics of Weir

1965/1966. Published here for the first time. Manuscript in Philip Lamantia Papers, 1944–2005, Bancroft Library, University of California, Berkeley [BANC MSS 2006/179].

It appears pure coincidence that Lamantia created and explored his highly imaginative concept of "weir" at about the same time a musician with that last name began playing rhythm guitar in a highly inventive way with a Bay Area band that became the Grateful Dead. Regardless, it remains true that Lamantia, in the words of the French critic Yves Le Pellec, was "a living link between French Surrealism and the American counterculture at its beginnings." (See Yves Le Pellec, "Un Surréaliste en Californie," in *Entretiens* 34 / Beat Generation (Paris: Editions Subervie, 1975), page 193.)

Testament of the Inter-Voice

1968. Unpublished in Lamantia's lifetime, this manuscript is a part of the Philip Lamantia Papers, 1944–2005, Bancroft Library, University of California, Berkeley [BANC MSS 2006/179], and in advance of the present collection appeared in *Seedings*, Issue Four (Fall 2017), pages 86–87.

Introduction to The Wounded Mattress *(1970) by Sotère Torregian*

Torregian, Sotère, *The Wounded Mattress* (Berkeley: Oyez, 1970).

The book's cover states, in addition to the author and title, "Introductory Note by Philip Lamantia." A facsimile of Lamantia's signature appears beneath the note.

The unnamed zoo twice referenced in the introduction's first paragraph, from which "the wild cry of the peacocks" is heard and where "wayward feathers" are hunted, must be Seattle's Woodland Park Zoo. Allusions to the "peacock" can be found in the poems "I Touch You" and "The Analog," both of which were written around the same time as this introduction. See *CPL* at pages 258 and 278.

Philip Lamantia

The New American Poetry Circuit (San Francisco: The New American Poetry Circuit, n.d. [1970]), n.p.

This pamphlet, with autobiographical or other statements written by various poets, was published by a poet's booking agency, self-described as "help[ing] colleges and universities to arrange readings by distinguished American poets."

The youthful fever-vision Lamantia mentions here, with its "apparition of a radiating blue-gowned woman," may be referenced in his poems "Descent," "The Call," "My Labyrinth," "Blue Grace," and "Blue Locus," which appear to allude to the fever-vision. See *CPL* at pages 50, 119, 139, 226, and 260.

Statement for Contemporary Poets of the English Language *(1970)*

Murphy, Rosalie, editor, *Contemporary Poets of the English Language* (New York: St. Martin's Press, 1970), page 625.

Between the Gulfs (with "By Elective Affinities, Then and Now")

Arsenal, No. 2 (Summer 1973: Chicago), page 32.

Reprinted, as separate works, in Rosemont, Franklin, Rosemont, Penelope, and Garon, Paul, editors, *The Forecast Is Hot!: Tracts & Other Collective Declarations of the Surrealist Movement in the United States 1966–1976* (Chicago: Black Swan Press,

1997), pages 184-185 and 193. "Between the Gulfs" alone was also reprinted in Sakolsky, Ron, editor, *Surrealist Subversions: Rants, Writings & Images by the Surrealist Movement in the United States* (Brooklyn: Autonomedia, 2002), page 183.

Vital Conflagrations

Bulletin of Surrealist Information, No. 4 (Chicago: no publisher, December 1973).

Reprinted thrice: *Surrealism: The Octopus-Typewriter*, No. 1 (October 1978), page 1; *Arsenal / Surrealist Subversion* 4 (1989: Chicago), page 30; and Rosemont, Franklin, Rosemont, Penelope, and Garon, Paul, editors, *The Forecast Is Hot!: Tracts & Other Collective Declarations of the Surrealist Movement in the United States 1966-1976* (Chicago: Black Swan Press, 1997), pages 194-195.

The Crime of Poetry

Ferlinghetti, Lawrence, editor, *City Lights Anthology* (San Francisco: City Lights Books, 1974), pages 249-250. The essay appears in a separate section titled "The Surrealist Movement in the U.S.," said to have been "entirely compiled and edited by members of the surrealist movement."

Harmonian Research

Ferlinghetti, Lawrence, editor, *City Lights Anthology* (San Francisco: City Lights Books, 1974), page 250.

This statement—more properly an invitation for readers to correspond about surrealism—is printed in a ruled box and, as with the essay above, appears in the separate "The Surrealist Movement in the U.S." section of the anthology. The invitation is uncredited, but the San Francisco post office box given (for "Magnetic Fields") is the same as listed for Lamantia in a boldly titled "Notice" printed directly below it. The "Notice," also printed in a ruled box, states:

Publishing projects *at the service of surrealism* are in formation, necessitating sympathetic and competent translations into English from French, Spanish, German, Portugeuse, Czech, and Slovakian, etc.

and lists Lamantia as the contact, at the same "Magnetic Fields" post office box listed at the end of "Harmonian Research."

Reprinted, with Lamantia explicitly credited as the author, in Rosemont, Franklin, Rosemont, Penelope, and Garon, Paul, editors, *The Forecast Is Hot!: Tracts & Other Collective Declarations of the Surrealist Movement in the United States 1966–1976* (Chicago: Black Swan Press, 1997), page 208.

The Oneiric Light of Alice Farley

Brides of the Prism (no place [San Francisco]: no publisher [Surrealist Movement in the United States], n.d. [June 1975]), n.p. [page 4].

A program for a performance of surrealist dance choreographed and performed by Farley at The Open Theater. In addition to a listing of production credits and dance titles, the program—12 pages counting the front and rear covers—also features a long poem by Laurence Weisberg, Farley's husband and Lamantia's friend and poet-associate.

Poetic Matters (with "Notes Toward a Rigorous Interpretation of Surrealist Occultation")

Arsenal, No. 3 (Spring 1976: Chicago), pages 6–10.

Three illustrations accompany the original publication: a large, above-the-title, historical black-and-white photo of a long parade of horses and riders captioned "Procession of Blackfoot Braves" and two small reproductions of drawings labeled "Ojibwa Pictographs" and "Zuni Hunting Fetish." It is not known whether Lamantia selected or approved these illustrations.

Reprinted without the illustrations, and as separate works with one given a variant title, in Sakolsky, Ron, editor, *Surrealist Subversions: Rants, Writings & Images by the Surrealist Movement in the United States* (Brooklyn: Autonomedia, 2002), pages 283–290 ("Poetic Matters: A Critique of the 'New American Poetics'") and 438–440 ("Notes Toward a Rigorous Interpretation of Surrealist Occultation").

Invisible Webs

Alice Farley: Surrealist Dance (Chicago: Gallery Black Swan, 1976), n.p.

Lamantia's comment is one of several similarly short statements or poems by various writers included in a program for performances done as part of the May 1976 World Surrealist Exhibition in Chicago.

Reprinted in *Surrealism: The Octopus-Typewriter*, No. 1 (October 1978), page 7.

Gerome Kamrowski: The Revelation of Night

Gerome Kamrowski: Then & Now (Chicago: Gallery 2269, 1976), n.p. The text as printed there had no title.

Reprinted, with the title used here, in Sakolsky, Ron, editor, *Surrealist Subversions: Rants, Writings & Images by the Surrealist Movement in the United States* (Brooklyn: Autonomedia, 2002), page 515.

Radio Voices: A Child's Bed of Sirens

Cultural Correspondence, No. 10–11 (Fall 1979: Providence, Rhode Island), pages 25–31.

As first published, the essay had several illustrations: a reproduction of seemingly original art, by an unidentified hand, neatly frames the title; there are also reproductions of three 1930s covers of the pulp magazine *The Shadow*, a drawing of Mandrake the Magician, three 1938 panels from the *Mandrake* comic strip, and a drawing captioned "The Shadow as drawn by Earl Mayan."

Reprinted in identical form in *Surrealism & Its Popular Accomplices* (San Francisco: City Lights, 1980), pages 25–31. Reprinted without illustrations in Sakolsky, Ron, editor, *Surrealist Subversions: Rants, Writings & Images by the Surrealist Movement in the United States* (Brooklyn: Autonomedia, 2002), pages 580–589. A slightly revised and redacted version was included in Buhle, Paul, editor, *Popular Culture in America* (Minneapolis, University of Minnesota Press: 1987), pages 139–149.

In this rich and vibrant essay, Lamantia—not surprisingly, given that it was based in part on memories of events then some 40 years in the past—errs on a few details. He names Victor Jory as the actor who portrayed the title character in the 1939 Columbia Pictures *Mandrake the Magician* movie serial, but Warren Hull played the part. Similarly, Lamantia near the end of his essay writes it was Mandrake who marvelously journeyed to a sub-atomic world within a coin, but it was Brick Bradford, of the eponymous daily sci-fi/fantasy newspaper comic strip created by William Ritt and Clarence Gray.

Lamantia was 10 and 11 years old when that particular *Brick Bradford* 288-strip sequence, known as "Adrift in an Atom" (or "Voyage in a Coin"), ran weekdays from February 8, 1937, to January 8, 1938. In 1976, a small English edition of the sequence was published in Papeete, Tahiti, of all places. Contemporary readers may thus read the comic adventure that so enthused Lamantia and, as he writes in the essay, was for his friends and acquaintances "the source of endless reveries at every chance turn in the long chain of phantasmagoric events."

The Future of Surrealism

Cultural Correspondence, No. 12–14 (Summer 1981: Providence, Rhode Island), pages 75–76.

This joint Lamantia-Nancy Peters statement is one of almost two dozen untitled mini-essays by various writers, presented under the general title "Symposium on Surrealism."

Reprinted, with the title used here, in Sakolsky, Ron, editor, *Surrealist Subversions: Rants, Writings & Images by the Surrealist Movement in the United States* (Brooklyn: Autonomedia, 2002) at pages 230–231.

Alice Farley: Dancing at Land's End

Buhle, Paul, et al., editors, *Free Spirits: Annals of the Insurgent Imagination* (San Francisco: City Lights, 1982) at page 81.

The page facing Lamantia's text features a full-page photo of Farley a-dancing atop Land's End in western San Francisco, with the surf and ocean below.

Reprinted without the photo in Sakolsky, Ron, editor, *Surrealist Subversions: Rants, Writings & Images by the Surrealist Movement in the United States* (Brooklyn: Autonomedia, 2002) at page 515.

Marie Wilson

Apparitions: Paintings and Drawings of Marie Wilson (San Francisco: City Lights, March 1984), n.p.

A brochure for an art exhibition. Fifteen years earlier, a reproduction of a Wilson drawing was used as the frontispiece for Lamantia's *The Blood of the Air* (San Francisco: Four Seasons Foundation, 1970).

Clark Ashton Smith Plaque Dedication

Published here for the first time. Manuscript in Philip Lamantia Papers, 1944–2005, Bancroft Library, University of California, Berkeley [BANC MSS 2006/179].

The poster for the dedication shows that the ceremony was held at the Auburn-Placer County Library at 1:00 p.m. on August 18, 1985, and, in addition to Lamantia, included Fritz Leiber and Donald Sidney-Fryer as speakers. It must have been a marvelous, fantastic, Spenserian afternoon.

Statement on "Howl"

Ginsberg, Allen, *Howl: Original Draft Facsimile, Transcript, and Variant Versions, Fully Annotated by Author [etc.]*, ed. Barry Miles (New York: Harper and Row, 1986) at page 124.

Ginsberg introduces Lamantia's statement by recounting that in the early 1950s Jack Kerouac told him about Lamantia's "celestial adventure." Lamantia also describes his adventure in two early 1960s poems, "Visions" and "Crystals." *CPL* at pages 125–126 (the prose paragraph beginning, "I remember the time . . .") and 147–149 (the final stanza).

Letter from Egypt

1989. Published here for the first time. Manuscript in Philip Lamantia Papers, 1944–2005, Bancroft Library, University of California, Berkeley [BANC MSS 2006/179].

Lamantia near the letter's start indicates that he'd been reading R. A. Schwaller de Lubicz's *The Temple of Man* for 25 years; this presumably was in the original French edition or a privately made translation. He later refers to "*The T.K.*," an abbreviation for Schwaller de Lubicz's *Les Temples de Karnak*, which features 600 photographs of the ancient site. He also references Schwaller de Lubicz's *Sacred Science: The King of Pharaonic Theocracy* (Inner Traditions, 1982, reprinted 1988) four times. The Bancroft Library's Lamantia Papers include his copies of texts from *Le Temple de l'Homme*, a privately made, "rough" translation of that book, his original French edition of *Les Temples de Karnak*, and his annotated copy of *Sacred Science*. In the late 1990s, Inner Traditions published English translations of *The Temple of Man* and *The Temples of Karnak*.

Preface to Crossroads of the Other *(1992)* by Ken Wainio

Wainio, Ken, *Crossroads of the Other* (Portland, OR: Locust Press & Record Company, 1992) [limited edition (20 copies) artist's book, "done in stone"]; (San Francisco: Androgyne Books, 1993) [trade edition].

A 14-line excerpt from the preface serves as a blurb on the trade edition's back cover. Lamantia's copy of the trade edition, inscribed to him by Wainio, is in the Bancroft Library at the University of California, Berkeley.

At the end of the preface's long final sentence, Lamantia alludes to "a true poet" who "announced not too long ago" that real life "'is absent.'" The reference is to Arthur Rimbaud's *A Season in Hell*.

Program Note from a Reading at the Poetry Project at St. Mark's Church, April 1999

Lamantia, writing about himself in the third person, typed the note single-spaced on one page, then had it faxed to the Poetry Project, which photocopied it and distributed copies to those who attended the April 21, 1999, reading.

Surrealism & Mysticism

2001. "Last Interview," in *Mirage #4/Period(ical)*, No. 121 (August 2005), n.p.

This is one of only approximately a half-dozen published interviews with Lamantia. The most extensive is in Meltzer, David, editor, *San Francisco Beat: Talking with the Poets* (San Francisco: City Lights Books, 2001), pages 133–149.

Statement

2001. "Last Interview," in *Mirage #4/Period(ical)*, No. 121 (August 2005), n.p.

ACKNOWLEDGMENTS

The editor would like to thank Nancy J. Peters, Philip Lamantia's literary executor, and Steve Fama, indefatigable bibliographer, for their collaboration on this project. Special thanks to all the people who read portions of this book in progress: Willie Alexander, Micah Ballard, Andrew Joron, Suzanne Kleid, Brian Lucas, Michael McClure, and Cedar Sigo. Thanks are due as well to Lawrence Ferlinghetti, Elaine Katzenberger, and the entire crew at City Lights Books, as well as to Penelope Rosemont and the Chicago Surrealists. Final thanks to the staff at Wave Books, especially Joshua Beckman, Heidi Broadhead, and Blyss Ervin.